MAYBE BABY

MAYBE BABY

ON THE
MOTHER SIDE

Kate Lawler

SEVEN DIALS

First published in Great Britain in 2022 by Seven Dials
an imprint of The Orion Publishing Group Ltd
Carmelite House, 50 Victoria Embankment
London EC4Y 0DZ

An Hachette UK Company

1 3 5 7 9 10 8 6 4 2

A CIP catalogue record for this book is
available from the British Library.

ISBN (Hardback) 978 1 3996 0236 5
ISBN (eBook) 978 1 3996 0238 9
ISBN (Audio) 978 1 3996 0239 6

Typeset by Input Data Services Ltd, Somerset

Printed in Great Britain by Clays Ltd, Elcograf S.p.A.

MIX
Paper from
responsible sources
FSC® C104740
FSC
www.fsc.org

www.orionbooks.co.uk

For Noa, you made me fall in love all over again.
And for Boj, I wouldn't be the mum I am
without you. x

Contents

Introduction   1

Chapter 1 – Maybe Not   3
Chapter 2 – Changing Times   27
Chapter 3 – Maybe Baby   41
Chapter 4 – Baby Steps   51
Chapter 5 – Labour and Pain   79
Chapter 6   Post-natal   91
Chapter 7 – Dark Times   109
Chapter 8 – Taking Steps   133
Chapter 9 – Silver Linings   151
Chapter 10 – Growing Up   173
Chapter 11 – The Big Firsts   189

Letter to Noa   239
Kate's Top Tips   245
Acknowledgements   255
About the Author   259

Introduction

Whether you've always wanted to be a parent or the idea of having a baby makes you break out into a cold sweat, whether you're a loving step-parent or you've given birth to your precious only child, whether you're surrounded by a whole bunch of kids or enjoying this in blissful solitude – or any other one of the hundred ways we live with and love other people – I hope you'll find something in this book.

I've always been completely honest about my baby-making decisions, giving birth, and everything that came after, and while it wasn't always brilliennnnnnt, I hope that by putting it all out *here* I might help someone out *there*.

I wish I'd known sooner that it could feel like this, both the good bits and the bad bits, and just remember: it's OK to need help sometimes.

It can get better,

Kate x

I

Maybe Not

If you ask anyone, they'll tell you that I've never been maternal. I know that's not the obvious choice for the start of a book about motherhood, but it's true. Of course I love my friends, but I've gotta be honest: I've never taken much of an interest in their kids. It goes without saying I've always been delighted for them (I'm not *that* much of a dick), but whenever I went to meet one of their babies for the first time, it went like this: 'D'you want to hold them?' they'd ask, to which I'd reply, 'Nah, you're all right, thanks.'

Every. Single. Time.

Of course, newborn babies are cute, but I just didn't have the desire to cuddle one. Puppies, yes. Babies, no. I had an irrational fear that I'd accidentally drop or hurt them, and presumed any baby would cry as soon as I picked them up. One time I held a newborn at arm's length for five seconds then said, 'OK, he's lovely, you can have him back now.' I was terrified. Friends would ask, 'D'you fancy changing a nappy?' and I'd politely decline thinking, *Why would I want to do that? No thank you. Not for me.* And when it came to babysitting, I'd always make my excuses. I've babysat *once* as an adult and spent the entire two hours staring at the monitor thinking, ***Please*** *don't wake up while I'm still here.*

Growing up I wasn't a girl who wanted to play with dolls, nor did I ever dream of the daughters and sons I'd have. I never, *ever* felt broody, I never saw babies and wanted one, I never even spoke about having kids, not even about possibly wanting them in the future.

Seeing friends with their children made me really happy for them, but in the back of my mind I was always thinking, *This life just isn't for me.* Even when my hedonistic raving days were behind me, I still wanted the freedom of being able to go to the pub or a gig after work if I felt like it, I enjoyed having the time and energy to go to the gym whenever and wherever, I was focused on my career, making money, doing what I wanted with my disposable income. I loved having weekends, mini-breaks and holidays to myself and despite being surrounded by more friends with children than ever before, I never once thought, *I wish that was me*, even in late 2018 when many of our friends were either parents already or trying for a baby. It felt like a mini baby boom within my friendship group, pregnancy announcements, births, most of which were wonderfully uncomplicated, another of which was so beautiful it made me cry when the video was sent to our 'Girl Talk' WhatsApp group. I sobbed as I watched one of my best friends in a birthing pool calmly push this teeny tiny human out of her vagina with just gas and air like an absolute warrior. All I could think was, *This is mind-blowing but I'm never, ever doing it, no chance, and if I do I certainly won't be quiet about it.* I'd be out for dinner with a friend and over a glass of wine she'd reveal that she was now trying for a baby as well, but not once did I get a twinge of broodiness. Instead, I was living happily child-free and announcing how thrilled we were to have welcomed another dog into our family. All I wanted was to be a dog mum. Some people are broody and maternal their entire life, and they totally love kids – even those that aren't their own – while for some of us, procreating is just not on our radar. Both are fine, I reckon.

When I first met Boj, I'd just come out of a really long-term relationship, and jumping straight into another one was of no interest to me. I'll always remember saying to him on our very first date, 'By the way, this isn't going anywhere. I'm not interested in marriage,

I'm not interested in kids, I'm not interested in settling down. This is just a bit of fun.' His first thought apparently was, *Calm down, love, we've only just met.* But look at him now. He's somehow got all three!

So time passed and I could feel myself falling for him, and we settled down with my dog, Baxter, and a rescue dog we adopted together, Shirley, making a home for the four of us in a little London flat. I remember saying to my friends that if I was ever gonna have kids, this is the man I would have kids with. I'd never said that about anyone. Subconsciously, I must have been thinking that if I was ever going to change my mind, I was finally in the right relationship for it.

And Boj kept asking. Every year I'd say, 'Maybe next year we can try for a baby, ask me again next year,' and every January he'd ask if I was ready, and I'd say, 'No, I'm still not ready.' It was hard for both of us, because it was something he wanted so much that was really important to him, but it was also something I'd been completely honest about from the start. He was asking for a bit of hope, but I had to remind him I'd never wanted what he was hoping for, and had told him that from our very first date. I don't think it makes me a bad person that I felt that way, and I don't believe you should ever apologise for your life choices. I loved my life, I loved my career, I loved what Boj and I had together, and I didn't feel ready to put all that aside for something that didn't even appeal to me in the first place. Sometimes I'd reflect on an argument we'd had over the subject and the internal battle would begin. Boj would make a great dad . . . But I love our life as it is now . . . But it'd be lovely to make a baby with the man I love . . . But why would I want to bring a baby into a world that's over-populated, the leader of the free world is Donald Trump, and climate change is a threat to humanity . . .? But look how much better things are here in the UK compared to a hundred years ago; we have electricity, our toilets are inside and our life expectancy is double, so perhaps things aren't so bad . . .? But *also* what if Boj falls out of love and leaves me with the baby? It was a far easier option to decide not to try for a baby, than to make probably the most important decision of my life to try and have one, so I left it at that.

My sisters had their kids quite young, in their twenties. I never babysat for them once – I mean, I feel quite bad about that now, obviously. Really bad. Sorry, you two! If you think that's bad, I couldn't even remember my nephews' birthdays until a few years ago, and I haven't always been the most involved auntie. I've always treated them at Christmas and birthdays, but when I was living in the north and the Midlands I'd never think, *Yay, I'm coming home to London to visit my nephews!* I'd be thinking, *Yay, I'm coming home to see my mum and dad, and my sisters and my brother.* But if any of them said to me now, 'Meh, I'm not that fussed about seeing Noa,' I'd be devastated! Although it would definitely be a little taste of karma for Auntie Kate. Ha!

I might sound really cold, I know. Quite a few people have said to me, 'Don't worry about it. All other kids are annoying apart from your own,' or 'I don't like other people's children, I just like my own.'

I was really surprised the first time I heard that – I thought it was just me. It's not just me, is it? It can be funny if your own child doinks herself on the head, but if you laugh at someone else's kid, and I'm sorry to say I have done, you're a *monster.* Even after Noa was born, I thought I was doing playdates all wrong, but I still don't see someone else's baby and think, *Ooooh let me have a cuddle!* I also still look at toddlers with snot and food all over their face, perhaps having a meltdown because they're not allowed another ice cream and think, *How do I get out of here?!* Then I realise that it's only a matter of time before I'm dealing with my own snotty-nosed, ice-cream-obsessed toddler. Brilliennnnnt. But show me a dog and I'm like a kid on Christmas Eve. I'm dog mad. I BLOODY LOVE 'EM! Can I stroke your dog? Can I give your dog a treat? Can I hug your dog? Let me walk your dog. *What a good boy.* Like I say, always room for more dogs.

Before Noa, I was more than happy with just dogs being my entire universe. I have two: Baxter is an eleven-year-old Border terrier, and Shirley was advertised as a Border terrier cross, but we did her DNA and she's apparently 25 per cent Chihuahua, 25 per cent Yorkshire terrier, 25 per cent Staffie, and 25 per cent sighthound, AKA a megamix! All I know is that if those two had to fend for themselves in the wild, Shirley would live until she was ancient with barely any teeth, crossing the rainbow bridge in her sleep, and Baxter would be dead within five minutes. Baxter is the most gentle, laid-back boy, who these days is quite happy to go for a walk, but equally happy to stay at home sleeping on our bed. Baxter in the summer is my favourite – he'll find a patch of sun inside our home and lie on the carpet panting like mad with his eyes closed, looking like a grandad dozing off in his armchair. Shirley, on the other hand, is much like her *Eastenders* namesake: rough, tough and ready for a fight with any cat, rat, fox or squirrel that dares to come within five feet of the back garden. She was somewhat jealous if we ever showed Baxter affection in front of her and very aggressive while out on walks during the first few months of her joining our family, so we knew it was Shirlz in particular who would need a great deal of training and extra special attention if any baby was to follow her into our pack.

One of the reasons I didn't want a baby for so long was these two: how could I possibly explain to them what was happening? You can get picture books for older siblings to understand the process of a baby arriving, and how their parents will still love them and all that, but all I could think of was Baxter and Shirley being pushed out by this new thing that didn't have four legs and a tail, and having no way to make them understand what was going on. Their whole lives would be transformed literally overnight, from me walking them as normal one day, to me being stuck on the sofa or in bed with this screaming new pack member they didn't ask for. I massively feared that I'd never be able to give them the attention they were used to, and they deserved.

When we were shooting *Celebrity Bumps* for MTV during my pregnancy, they asked if we'd still make a fuss of them, if they'd still get birthday celebrations once Noa was in the picture. I didn't even hesitate: 'Absolutely!' I said, with confidence and conviction. But now I understand why they asked that question, because it was Baxter's eleventh birthday on 2 November and, for the first time ever, he didn't get his annual birthday steak for tea. I had every intention, but by the time we cooked it for him it was – wait for it – 9 November! I realise Baxter had absolutely no idea he'd missed out on a steak for his birthday, and of course we still made a fuss of him on the day, but since having a baby I never manage to do anything when I say I'm going to do it.

That said, I promised myself the dogs would never be pushed aside once Noa arrived, and it's a promise I'm pleased to say I've kept. We include Baxter and Shirley in everything we possibly can with Noa and as a result I can already tell she's going to be a dog person, especially when I see her with Baxter – they're such a cute pair already. He follows us everywhere because he wants to be where Noa is. He trots up the stairs behind us every evening to observe bath time and when Boj or I run the bath, he'll sit by her side in the nursery as if he's guarding her. He drops his toys in front of her all the time, and while she isn't quite able to throw one for him to fetch, she laughs out loud watching Baxter and I play tug of-war with a squeaky hedgehog or rubber chicken. He used to rest his head on my tummy when Noa was in there and I like to think it's because he knew his Mummy was growing something tremendously precious that he wanted to protect. I can't wait until Noa is old enough to walk him on the lead, I just hope he sticks around long enough for that to happen. I can't bear the thought of one day having to have a conversation with Noa about why the dogs she's grown up with aren't around any more. Baxter's her best friend right now.

For the first six months after Noa was born, though, that was another part of my guilt. People who aren't dog people really struggle to understand this, but Baxter and Shirley *were* my kids, they still *are* my kids. They've never been pets, I've never been their owner, they're two members of our family, Noa's big brother and sister, and now I wasn't able to walk them, play with them, even come down in the mornings and feed them. I couldn't pick them up for a long time because of my lower abdomen healing from birth, and dogs give you the saddest look even at the best of times, but this would make me sob. What had I done? I'd already been kept away from them for five long days while Noa and I were in hospital, and now everything had been turned completely upside down. It didn't help when *Daily Mail* commenters decided to annihilate me when I posted a picture of me and the dogs on Mother's Day. But that's who the dogs are to me – I'm their *mother*, I've never been their *owner*, and at that time, they were the only kids I felt like I knew, I understood, who I wasn't crying over every day, and the guilt I had for feeling like I'd abandoned Baxter and Shirley prompted me to share that photo of us on social media, I guess.

Plenty of people have said to me, 'You must have known you were going to have a baby when you did the first series of your podcast?' And I really didn't. I was still completely on the fence, and by then I'd been ambivalent for a while.

Podcasting with Boj looked like a lot of fun, but we didn't want to just do a podcast for the sake of it. Then I realised what a unique position we were in: with almost every other heterosexual couple we knew that didn't have kids, it was the women who really wanted to start trying and the men who were keen to wait a little longer and pushing back. We ended up doing the podcast because we genuinely wanted to know as much as we could about the whole thing, hearing every side of the argument, getting all the facts before we even thought about making a decision. I was also approaching my forties, which meant it might not have even been possible for me, so we needed to find out if both Boj and I were able to have children.

The conversations on series one of *Maybe Baby* really helped, listening to all of our guests telling their truth about having kids – or not having them. Jenny Eclair was absolutely brilliant, talking about the joys of having her daughter at twenty-eight, and how she raised Phoebe with her husband and with the nanny who's still very close to the family, and how having that 'second mother' made her daughter so stable and happy; Jenny's also promised to babysit, so, Jenny, if you're reading this, CALL ME.

Jenny spoke so eloquently too, not only about having to milk herself into a loo after her daughter's birth, but also about the overwhelming fear she's always felt as a mother, and how that was part of why they only ever had one child. She says even these days, if her daughter calls, she's convinced it's because she's in danger or something terrible has happened. I can totally relate to that now and as much as I try, I know that fear is only going to amplify as Noa gets older.

Angela Barnes was hilarious and honest about her choice to be childfree, summing up perfectly my feelings about how people seem to think both your feelings for the planet and your relationship with your partner must somehow be less if you don't have a kid – 'Only parents can really understand worrying about the future. If you don't want a baby together, it's obvious that you don't love each other enough.' This is complete rubbish. Angela and I also shared worries about the stress babies bring to a relationship: if you really love each other and are happy, why add something into the mix to mess with it? We talked with her about how there's no point having kids just because of FOMO, or because they'll be company when you're old, and how there's plenty of elderly parents who never hear from their kids. At least with dogs they respect your hangovers.

I really enjoyed that episode with Angela, and I look back at the series and wish we'd recorded more episodes with people who were child-free. Maybe the whole series was a bit one-sided because that part of me was already edging over into a decision, even if I didn't realise it or wasn't ready to admit it yet. Every other guest would say, more or less, 'Babies are great and having them is the best thing we've ever done, you should do it, it will improve your life in every way!' Or maybe I thought that, since my anti-baby opinion was so strong, me having all those pro-baby people was balancing out my own feelings. Speaking to Angela, there was a moment where she talked about finally meeting someone she wanted to spend the rest of her life with, and he didn't want children either; it made me wonder whether, if her partner had wanted kids as much as Boj did, she would ever have changed her mind? It took seven years with Boj for me to finally be ready – even though some online commenters were convinced at the time that Boj forced me into it! – and it made me wonder: if women's eggs were infinite and we remained fertile for much, much longer, would more women eventually choose to have children? Maybe we would have our years of going out and having careers, and women like me might have waited just a little bit longer, but still would have had a baby at the end of it.

Spencer Matthews and Vogue Williams, only on their first then but now expecting their third child, talked about how their son was suctioned out with a ventouse and had such an extremely misshapen head for a while that no family members even responded to the extremely ugly baby photos they sent out. Spencer also promised us that babies sleep twenty hours a day, and said, 'If you want some rest, your best bet is to have a baby.' Spencer, you and I need a word, mate.

The Scummy Mummies were fantastic, sharing their totally different baby feelings and pregnancy experiences, from being broody as a child and spending the pregnancy talking to the bump, to the distress of having a two-month-premature baby. I look back on that latter conversation so differently now, having my own experience of a tiny baby in the NICU. They also promised pregnancy would deliver huge boobs, great hair, and great skin, and taught us about doulas, the back-up maternity support you can hire privately to help you through birth and the following days or weeks. Helen sang the praises of home births in water pools so much that I almost considered it, and she pointed out the madness of women getting massive support during labour, just before being chucked out on day one of their baby's life and being told to get on with it alone. Totally mad.

My lovely friend Alison Hammond from my *Big Brother* days talked to us about her five-day induction – I think Boj is still in shock at googling a 'sweep' – and her C-section. I don't think I had ever thought of it as surgery before, and what a major operation it actually is, and Alison also made us think about best- and worse-case scenarios for how a relationship can change when a baby joins it.

Russell Kane gave us tips on sleep routines and staying connected as a couple, and how he didn't feel a bond with his daughter until she became a 'psychopathic bastard' two-and-a-half-year-old toddler; Bryony Gordon talked to us about parenting through her mental illness, and recommended as her tip for every potential parent to 'sort your shit out' with good therapy in order to not pass issues down to any children, Boj's mum, Sue, shared how different birth was even forty years ago, and how much child-rearing philosophies have changed around feeding and sleeping on demand. She told us how she didn't sleep for *five years* during the early stages of Boj and his sister, which makes me think she's even more of a wonder woman. She also said Boj's head was so big that if he was her first child she'd never have had another one. She had to keep taking Boj for regular check-ups, and it was only after a year that the hospital confirmed he probably just had a big old brain. And that turned out to be true, right, Boj?

They all gave us such useful insights into parenting, not parenting, and what those choices could mean for our future, and Boj made plenty of helpful observations, too. Not least that maybe I was just scared of committing to something I would live with for the *rest* of my life, no quitting like a job, no divorcing like a spouse, no moving away like a bad property; maybe I just needed to have my mind made up for me by circumstances, so I'd stop having to worry about the pressure of a decision. (Spoiler: thanks, COVID-19.) But the conversation that really swung the needle was the one we had with Dr Marie Wren, deputy director at The Lister, one of London's leading fertility clinics. She checked us both out, and revealed that while Boj's sperm looked pretty good, my eggs were in definite decline and I shouldn't put having a baby 'on the back burner for two years'. I knew I wasn't getting any younger, but somehow hearing her talk about it so starkly was a shock, and I actually started crying. I didn't necessarily have the choices I thought I did. She was very reassuring, reminding me that I wasn't infertile and that there was nothing to indicate there would be a problem with getting pregnant, but if we were thinking about it, sooner was better than later.

I must have, on some level, been getting myself ready for having our own baby, and the final switch flipped when Boj asked me to marry him. The podcast episode at the fertility clinic had taken me by surprise and left me feeling worried for two reasons. Firstly, up until then I had a choice of whether to try for a baby or not. I was in control and wanting to live child-free, even when I discussed the idea and entertained it for a while but remained undecided, and perhaps this was very naive of me; I felt safe in the knowledge that I had more than enough time to have a child if I changed my mind. Suddenly it began to dawn on me that very soon, I wouldn't have the luxury of waiting or debating, or even trying, because biologically it wouldn't be possible any more. Secondly, finding out I didn't have many eggs remaining made me think, *What if I wait until I'm forty and they're all gone? What if Boj and I try for a year and nothing? Will he still want to be with someone who can't give him a child?* One of my friends in a serious relationship recently found out she's gone through the menopause. She really, really wanted a baby, found a loving partner who wanted kids too, went to the doctors where they suspected the issue was depression, but found out instead that that was it: no more eggs. I saw how heartbroken she was and it broke me too, as she'd finally met the person she wanted to spend forever with, the man she wanted to make babies with. It was such a shock because she was only in her late thirties. Now she's waiting for a donor, because that's her best option.

I still get regular messages on Instagram from the parentally undecided, asking me what I think they should do, and I'm not going to lie. During the first nine months of Noa's life, I said to a few people who were completely 50/50 on having a child, 'If you are genuinely happy with your life right now and don't feel like you're missing out on anything every day, you're content and so is your partner, but you just feel like you *should* have a baby because society still expects you to, then don't do it.' In hindsight, during the first nine months of motherhood, I shouldn't have been giving anyone advice on whether or not to procreate, as my head was a complete mess. Ask me now and I'd probably have a very different answer. Once Noa reached nine months, a cloud slowly began to lift and I started to feel what everyone promised me I would feel (eventually). It was as if the old me was returning – albeit a new version – and despite missing the old Kate, carefree Kate, silly, funny, not-taking-life-too-seriously Kate, and certainly not depressed, anxious, angry Kate, I'm actually learning to love and accept the new me. I'm Kate Version 2.0, I love my daughter to the ends of the earth and would do absolutely anything for her. I also didn't think it was possible but I've even more love and admiration for Boj now that he's the father of our daughter – watching him with Noa and how they are together, I could melt. As Kate Version 2.0, my future has done a complete 180 and there are so many more exciting things to think about, like Noa's first Christmas, her first birthday, first day at nursery, first day at school, holidays we'll have together, adventures we'll go on together, her first boyfriend or girlfriend, her first job! Not only am I learning about her every day, I've learnt that my priorities in life have completely changed and it's OK to sometimes miss who I was before I had Noa. It's OK to have days where you feel trapped, anxious, overwhelmed, annoyed or resentful, because every day is different and your feelings change as quickly as your children do. Perhaps when she's older, I'll be convinced that everyone should have a child and it's the best thing ever, but for now I'm a grateful mother *and* a child-free advocate. Ultimately, it's not my decision for anyone else, but it's also important for women to fully understand that, unfair as it is, we don't have the chance to wait and live our lives doing all the things we want to do, because with age, it does often become much harder. And if I hadn't fallen pregnant first, second or fifteenth time and we'd needed to try IVF, maybe I'd be recommending women try much earlier – it's hard to give advice when there are so many different aspects to consider for every potential mum.

But I do know that I've always had so much love to give. I've been a great mum to the doggies because of how much time I've invested in making their lives enjoyable, and because I love them so much (too much, maybe), I cuddle and kiss them and have always treated them like miniature humans – hence their nickname, 'The Miniatures'. Because of this, I know I would have loved any child I had earlier on in life. I definitely would have had more energy being a younger mum, with less aches, pains and far fewer osteo appointments than I have now, but I don't think I would have been able to put my all into it because I simply wasn't ready and I didn't have the life experience I have now. I've learned so much from watching my friends have children, and seeing how it affected their lives and relationships, and whatever extra energy I might have had in my twenties, I wouldn't have been able mentally to go all-in on being a mum like I can now and really enjoy it, because I would have been too aware of all the stuff I was missing out on that for me was really important. For me, my twenties were a crazy, raucous, irresponsible wild ride and I loved every minute of it. I look back on that decade and wonder how I'm still alive, but I've some hilarious stories to tell Noa when she's old enough and

I don't regret anything I did, because I got it all out of my system in time to finally feel ready to settle down. I wouldn't have wanted to parent on a hangover, or be worrying about babysitters while I flew abroad to DJ. At twenty-eight, I was out every single weekend, and it was about going out, getting drunk, having a good time and not caring about anyone else but me. Kind of selfish, but a lot of fun.

Too many people – including me – have had to deal with nosy questions about when they're going to have kids, or a raised eyebrow when they've said they don't want them yet. How do other adults not realise how rude that is? How do they know what that person's circumstance is? For many, it's a delicate and upsetting question to be asked. And really, the only acceptable answer to those asking is, 'I'm pregnant already,' because if you explain you and your partner are trying and it's not happened yet, it can be incredibly awkward, especially if you feel uncomfortable talking about the fertility journey you're on. And if you say, 'Oh no, we don't want them,' then people are gobsmacked and won't actually believe that you could feel that way. How can it be possible that a woman doesn't want children? Sometimes you just can't win. And that needs to change.

In fact, the only correct answer to that question is simple: 'Mind your own business.'

I look at Noa now and find it absolutely fascinating that I can see both me and Boj in her, that we made this person together. Boj says it's made us even closer, which makes me laugh because since Noa's arrival, our relationship has been pushed to its limits and at times it felt like we were drifting apart. He's seen me sob, moan and cry more in the past year than in the seven years prior combined, but I also get what he says: we'll be tied together forever by this wonderful little human being who will be there through our whole life, a bond that makes both of us want to be better people. On the other hand, I've got so many friends who are blissfully happy without children, and having been there I believe them and am so happy for them. I see that it's often women who struggle to understand that a happy child-free life can happen: that you can choose to be without a child and still have a great, fulfilling, joyful life. That you can understand love and empathy, even if you haven't given birth.

I disagree so strongly with that idea that only having a child shows you what 'real love' is. When I was child-free I knew exactly what real love was, and it varied, from the love I had for my family and friends, to the dogs, and Boj of course. The love I have for Noa is unbelievable and getting stronger by the day, but I can hand on heart say I knew what real love was before I had her.

When someone asks me if I love the dogs or Noa more, I can swear to them that I love them all equally. Noa is more fascinating, changing and growing and doing new things all the time, and I'm incredibly protective of her and worried about what she might come across in the world, and the dogs can't have conversations with me, nor can I make them laugh . . . but Noa will leave home one day, and have her own life, whereas Shirley and Baxter will always be with me, they'll never learn to open the fridge and make a sandwich or get a job. They're going to depend on me always and I know that I'll be their best friend until they eventually cross the rainbow bridge. I know people might think that's weird, but I don't think we should have to make excuses for inviting more love into our lives. We are a really happy family of five, and that can't be a bad thing, can it? You find happiness where you can. Should you be made to grieve what you haven't chosen? No, of course not. Society needs to let us make our choices and be OK with them.

What matters is being able to talk about what you want and what you don't want when it comes to kids. There's no right answer, obviously, and it's about what works for you. As long as you're not hurting anyone, and you're being honest with your partner, any choice you make is OK, but there's no point you and your partner being on completely different pages – Boj has said that we'd still be together even if I hadn't changed my mind, but I don't always know if that's true. I think he wants to believe it, but I suspect it would have got to the stage in our relationship where it was too much for him. After all, our opposing views on kids were already causing tension after a few years together. I know that if I wasn't with Boj, I wouldn't have had a baby, because with anyone else I've ever been with kids weren't on my agenda and that was that. Had Boj not wanted children either, we'd most probably have three dogs by now. Without Boj, I'd probably have ended up with ten Border terriers. At least.

2

Changing Times

So things started changing in 2018 when Boj proposed. I'd been putting him off since our first date, but recently had started wondering if maybe a proposal was on his mind. We'd been to Norway on a winter safari for his birthday, and at one point during the trip we found ourselves driving through the middle of the mountains at night, in search of the Northern Lights. It was pitch black until suddenly we spotted the most magical colours in the sky out of the window, so we stopped the car. The Northern Lights appeared and were *stunning*. It was the most perfect moment, where we were sharing a flask of hot chocolate and whiskey standing in the snow, watching the lights with not a single person around for miles, and I had a sudden thought: *I feel like he's going to propose.*

Then I thought, *Why are you thinking that, Lawler?*

Then I thought, *Oh my god, maybe I* want *him to propose.*

Then . . . no proposal. We've all had that moment where we get really hyped up about something, only then it doesn't bloody happen at all, but it did start something ticking in the back of my mind. Why had a proposal been my first thought?

A few months after that, I'd abandoned the idea of getting engaged. I'd always made it clear to Boj that I didn't want marriage, and nothing seemed to indicate it was on the horizon. We'd gone to Bruges for a weekend away, a trip I'd planned myself last minute so of course it felt even more like nothing was going to happen. It was just the two of us and Baxter, my beloved Border terrier, and I hadn't bothered to spray tan, my nail varnish was chipped and my roots should have been done before the mini-break. Classic Kate. Boj had asked me to pack a really nice outfit for one night, but he always found us a great restaurant to visit wherever we went, so again, I didn't think anything of it. What I didn't know was that this was the year he was planning to propose and the ring he'd chosen – with the intention of asking me later in 2018 – was ready sooner than he'd thought, and I definitely didn't know that he'd already asked my dad's permission, had brought the ring to Bruges, and planned to pop the question in the most romantic setting. Which I ruined.

At dinner the first night, we went to this really grand restaurant in a lovely old historic building. The guy at reception said, 'The dining room is through there. May I take your coats?'

Boj looked at the open cloakroom, near to the street door, and looked at the tables, through another door further into the building, and said, 'Oh . . . no . . . I'll . . . just keep my coat on me?' There was a brief verbal tussle, Boj thinking that it was probably a bit risky leaving the diamond ring in his pocket near an open door to the street, and the restaurant guy wondering why this mad tourist was insisting on eating his dinner wearing a heavy winter coat. Eventually Boj gave in. The meal was delicious, and I didn't have a clue that for the entire time, Boj was secretly shitting himself that the ring would get nicked. When we finished eating, he suggested a walk to the Bridge of Love nearby – apparently one of the most romantic spots in Bruges. I never found out more about it because without thinking, I said, 'Ahh, are you going to propose to me, babes?'

Boj spluttered, 'No!' and I said, 'Great! Let's go to a gin bar instead.'

As we walked along the cute cobbled streets of this beautiful city, I suddenly thought again, *Oh no!* Was *he about to propose?* I put my arm around his waist then gently put my hand inside his coat pocket to check if there was a ring box, and that's when he asked what the fuck I was up to.

'Nothing! Just . . . my hands are cold!' I put my hand in his pocket and was still rooting about – not realising it was actually in the inside pocket of his coat. Thinking about it now I realise what a dick move that was. If I'd found the ring I'd have totally ruined the surprise. Again: classic Kate.

We went to the gin bar, had fun, got trashed, and the next day we took Baxter to a beautiful beach at Knokke. It was a gorgeous sunny day, and I suggested we walk down the beach to one of the bars. Boj said, 'Shall we just sit down for a minute?'

I checked my step-count. 'Nah, I haven't done my ten thousand steps yet. And there's a lovely Aperol bar at the end there, look!'

'But . . . let's just sit for a minute. The three of us. Take it all in.'

'No, Boj, let's walk, Aperol spritz, then sit!'

He didn't actually say *For fuck's sake, Katie*, out loud, but looking back he was giving off seriously frustrated vibes, the poor handsome chap. So he couldn't propose on the beach, and when we got to the beach bar it was so rammed that he knew it wouldn't go down well if he tried it in front of so many people.

On the way back to Bruges, we stopped to get petrol, and while I waited in the car with Baxter, Boj bought a bottle of champagne from some weirdly nice petrol station, and stuffed it in his backpack. He'd resolved to ask me as soon as we got back to the hotel, because he didn't want to ask me on our last day, but when we got to our room I insisted on a nap.

When I woke up later, mascara in big black circles, Baxter snuggling up to me with death breath in my face, I opened my eyes to see Boj down on his knees, watching me.

'I've been meaning to ask you something.'

I was still half asleep. 'Wait . . . what are you doing?'

'I've been meaning to ask you a question for the last two days. But you fucked it up both times. You could have had a really romantic proposal last night. You could have had a romantic proposal today, but I do want to marry you. Will you marry me?'

'Oh my god,' I replied. 'I look like shit. Why are you proposing to me in bed like this?'

He pointed out again that he'd tried to propose on the bridge the night before, and I'd said no – but this time I said yes, and we were soon opening the champagne, FaceTiming our families and showing them the ring, which fit perfectly straightaway.

I asked him if he'd asked my dad, and he told me when we'd all been together at a family pub lunch recently while my mum and sisters and I were all chatting away, he'd strolled over to my dad at the bar and told him that he really loved me, and wanted to ask me to marry him.

Apparently Dad had paused for a moment, then said, 'Do you think she'll say yes?'

Boj said, 'I hope so,' and Dad finished the emotional heart-to-heart with his usual, 'Well . . . good luck to ya.'

But he'd asked me now, even though he knew I didn't want children, and I felt like he was really accepting me for who I was. Two years later I turned forty, and there was this sudden feeling of a snap decision happening, and I said to Boj that I was ready to try. The trouble was, I said we should start trying on our honeymoon, right after our June 2020 wedding. He was still taking it all with a pinch of salt, because I'd promised him soon, soon, soon, all those times, but I had it clear in my head: 'We're going to go to the Seychelles. I promise you, we'll start trying on our honeymoon. I know I'm going to be ready.'

Then the pandemic hit, and I realised our wedding was, to put it politely, fucked.

I was forty, facing the end of what felt like my child-bearing years (although I actually know plenty of women who've got pregnant in their forties), with a cancelled wedding, a cancelled honeymoon and the memory of a fertility clinic over a year ago gently telling me to maybe hurry it up if I wanted a baby. My concern was that if we'd pushed back the wedding another year and only started trying after that, would my fertile days have already gone? Then I thought, *What if it's not meant to be?* I'd spent so long without having a baby, and without wanting a baby; my life was shaped around my independence and all the things that go with it. I could do the jobs I wanted, go out when I wanted, see friends when I wanted. Was I too used to it all to share my life with a baby?

We spent the whole of May debating whether or not to try now in lockdown, going back and forth about timings and whether we could squeeze it in before our new wedding date in June 2021. I was determined not to be pregnant at our wedding (the one thing I knew was that it didn't have to be big, it didn't have to be grand, but I wanted to be able to drink as many cocktails as I fancied), so eventually I said, 'Should we just try it?' Boj was stunned. 'Everyone keeps suggesting it,' I said, 'that we should try and squeeze a baby in before the wedding. If we got pregnant this month, we've got nine months of being pregnant, then I'll have three months to get back into my dress!' (I look back on this now, as a mum, and wonder what the heck I was thinking. Three months? I could barely *speak* three months after having Noa, let alone get into the mood or shape to be wearing a wedding dress.) 'We wouldn't want a baby any younger than three months – three months and we'll be nailing it, won't we? It'll be easy as anything by then. Right, we've got one month. Let's just do it. Let's try, and if we're meant to have a baby before we marry, we will.'

We'd had these conversations before, although the first time round they were really difficult: where we were going, what we both wanted. And this wouldn't be the first time Boj and I had been pregnant. About three years into the relationship, in 2017, I got a positive pregnancy test. We were already living together, we'd just bought a flat together, we were definitely going all the way as a couple, but when I saw that line on the pregnancy test I started crying my eyes out, and I was beyond panicking. Boj was so calm, and just said, 'It doesn't matter, it's OK if you're not ready, let's not have a baby.'

Even the next day, I was still in panic mode. I sent him a message, saying, 'Are you 100 per cent OK with me getting an abortion? You won't hate me, will you?'

Boj replied, 'I would never hate you. Any decision about having a kid is huge. I don't underestimate it at all. Even though I'm obviously pro, for what it's worth, I don't think this is the right time.'

We both knew it was the right decision – we were living in a small flat and didn't have much space, I'd only just started working at Virgin Radio and I certainly wasn't in the right headspace to be pregnant or raising a baby. I felt physically sick at the thought of having to do it. When I arranged the abortion, the people at the clinic wanted to get to the bottom of the situation, to try to find out why I didn't want to be pregnant, why now was not the right time. And they also remind you that any abortion might affect your chances of getting pregnant in the future, which was a risk I was willing to take because, even at thirty-seven, I wasn't ready and it was only a small risk.

They were really sympathetic and explained what was going to happen, because I wasn't far gone at all. They gave me a tablet to take there, and a second tablet to take at home, which is the one that forces a miscarriage, and it's painful, and it's really horrendous when you're sitting on the toilet and a kind of sac comes out, which is the worst bit. I cried when I knew I had to flush the chain; I couldn't bring myself to do it for what felt like forever, but it must have only been around a minute. All I could think was, *That's it. That's what could have been.*

It's horrible – at that point I started thinking about the millions of women who go through the agony of mis-carriage or pregnancy loss, and I felt tremendous guilt that I was choosing to do this. It made me feel deeply sad that I was terminating a possible life, a life I'd made with the man I love, but it made me sadder for those women out there who've had fertility journeys lasting years, who never even got the chance to conceive, or have a viable pregnancy. I felt awful for some time after this and having carried Noa for nine months, I often think about what that little embryo might have become. Would it have been a boy or a girl? What would our lives have been like going through with a pregnancy I didn't want and was in no way ready for? I try not to think about it as it makes me sad, but I know I made the right choice and I'm grateful I had it. Even with the guilt, I'm such a firm believer that all women should have the choice, because if it's not right for you, you need to have that option, and I would have felt a million times worse if I'd have been forced to continue with something that I so strongly didn't want.

I felt horrific that whole weekend. I couldn't walk the dogs, I couldn't stop crying. It was a combination of the situation and the hormones, and I was still in pain. I kept worrying that this was a sign I would never, ever be ready for a baby, and I felt so sad, only wanting to watch TV and cuddle up with Boj, but he was so under-standing throughout the whole thing. I really thought he'd think that this was the perfect opportunity he'd been waiting so long for, but he never once gave any indication that was how he felt, he just looked after me.

About a fortnight afterwards, I was out for drinks with a friend, and she said, 'Oh, hang on, I need to go to the chemist, I need to get some sanitary towels.' And I said, 'Why are you wearing *sanitary towels?*' (We're good enough mates to know which period products we use.)

She paused for a moment then said, 'I've just had an abortion,' and I said, 'Are you joking? So have I,' and the pair of us were just looking at each other. We're both mums now, but I couldn't quite believe that both of us had accidentally fallen pregnant at the same time. We spoke that evening about our decisions to take the path we did, and it was obvious that neither of us were remotely in the right place to raise a baby.

And nothing really changed until Boj and I started doing our podcast, and a little thing called COVID-19 arrived.

I don't know how it happened – well, I mean, I do know, I'm an adult woman – but as soon as we decided to try for a baby, we got lucky straight away.

I'd been using an ovulation tracker to not get pregnant, but now I used it to track my most fertile stages in my cycle. I always get a pain when I'm ovulating, which turns out is really helpful when you're trying to get a bun in the oven. If you're trying to get pregnant and you get that pain, like a twinge on one side at a regular point in your cycle, that could be ovulation, and that's the time you need to get on the phone and get your partner home, tell them it's time to do it. Apparently it's even better if you have sex the day before, so some of the sperm are still hanging around in there when you're ovulating as they live for around five days, but as close as you can to ovulation is good. My app said my highest chance was on the Friday, but on Saturday I got the pain, and broke it to Boj that we'd have to do it again. And as soon as we did it, I just knew. I knew I was pregnant.

So much around pregnancy is just luck. One of my friends was on her IVF journey but had to stop for the pandemic, and then she ended up getting pregnant naturally during the lockdown despite believing she couldn't. I know others that have gone for that one last holiday before IVF and come home pregnant. It's easy to say, 'Try not to worry about it,' but when you've been trying for a while, it can seem like pregnant women are everywhere and it's impossible to think about anything else, and sex can start to become this awkward, scheduled thing. I think apps are great for tracking, initially, before getting professional medical support after a certain point – but it is still luck, like whether you live in an area where you can access free fertility treatment or how many cycles you're offered. Getting pregnant requires the patience of a saint from day one of trying – there's lots of waiting around for ovulation days, missed periods, the next ovulation days – and if you're success-ful with a pregnancy, that patience is key for when the hormones rage and everyone needs to cope with the madness that follows.

I did the pregnancy test without Boj, when it was time. I had every intention of doing it together, but he was taking ages to get ready and I knew there was a test sitting in the cupboard. I had such a strong feeling so I just did it and there it was: the line. *Pregnant.* And I thought: *Holy shitballs!* I knew I should have told him straightaway, but I panicked and didn't know how to say it; I think I also wanted to let it sink in, and process that I was pregnant without reaction from anyone else.

We went to lunch with friends that day, and all I could think was, *I can't believe I'm pregnant.* Oddly, that day they asked me if I'd thought any more about having children, and I just said, 'Oh, we've decided to try on honeymoon, after the wedding,' then changed the sub-ject. (Even more oddly, my *Big Brother* pal Alison Ham-mond called me that very night on FaceTime and said she'd had a dream the night before that I was pregnant

– I had to hide my face and end the call shortly after so she wouldn't guess the truth. How weird is that?) I was so nervous about telling Boj and for some reason I felt embarrassed and didn't know how to break the news to him. When we got back that night, Boj was chatting away – probably reminding me that I'd forgotten to pay money into our joint account again – as we got ready for bed, and I chucked the test at him. He was looking at it, then at me, then at the test, and eventually said, 'What does this mean? I've never seen a pregnancy test. Are you pregnant? How are you telling me like this? Are you joking?'

Payback for the proposal, mate. I was so happy and so excited though. This time, I knew I was completely ready.

3

Maybe Baby

One of the many things that had always put me off having a baby myself was the experiences the women around me had had. My mum gave birth to my elder sister, Kelly, in 1977, and tried originally to have a vaginal birth, but her pelvis was too small and she had to have an emergency C-section. Back then, if you had a C-section, you were fully put to sleep. So she went under, after a traumatising first go at a vaginal birth, then was woken later by a nurse telling her she'd had a daughter.

When she fell pregnant with me and Karen, they said, 'Given your previous birth, we don't really want to take any chances with twins, so you'll need to have a C-section; we'll do a planned one this time.' Once again she was put to sleep, woken up, then told she'd got twin daughters. That time I think she was a bit more fazed by the whole thing – she says now that she didn't like us two at all to begin with, which I find hilarious. Thanks, Mum! She asked the nurses to take us away, and it took about twenty-four hours before she started warming to us. But how must that feel, to wake up to the mushed-up faces of these pulled-out babies, when she didn't even know what sex we were going to be, and then told she had two more daughters – it's mad, isn't it? I don't think I would opt to go under full anaesthetic for a birth now, if I had a choice.

One of the good things then, though, was the fact that you'd be in hospital for a week after you had your baby, which I think should still be an option for those who want it. My mum had around the clock help with breastfeeding and other issues that always come up with newborns, and she learned so much from all the nurses and midwives in that time. She also had a proper opportunity to recover, because all she could do was lie in bed. If she was back at home I'm sure it would have been tempting to just stick the laundry on, do a quick bit of tidying, try and move about as normal.

When I first got back from hospital with Noa, Boj caught me trying to manage a full mountain of laundry.

'What are you doing?' he said.

I continued my slow walk with the dirty clothes. 'It's fine,' I said, wincing, 'I'm going really slow.'

Even though I'd been in hospital for five days, and technically it was allowed, Boj wrestled the laundry out of my hands and sent me back to the sofa.

I'm so physically like my mum that I assumed any attempt at a vaginal birth would be the same as hers: if I had a baby and tried to push it out, it would most probably result in a medical intervention anyway, so I decided I may as well take control and ask for an elective C-section from the very start. I pictured (too much) an emergency happening otherwise, and risking me or the baby – or both of us – dying. Everything about that terrified me, not having any idea at all what the challenges could be and how it could go wrong.

On top of that, I'd been at one of the labours of my twin, and she'd been pushing for ages until the midwife said, 'It's here! The head's here!' I ran down to have a look, instantly felt sick, but was totally fascinated as well. Then the midwife said, 'OK, we're going to need suction,' and suddenly my sister was shouting, 'I don't want a cone-head baby! Don't let my baby have a cone head!' and some giant scissors were being brandished.

The image of the midwife just coming at her with a pair of episiotomy scissors and just going *snip!*, just like she was cutting the string off a piece of lamb . . . It scarred me. I definitely had some post-traumatic stuff going on after watching my twin getting cut, and then getting stitched again, trying to wash, trying to wee, all the complications that can come for days or weeks after ... Another really good friend had a traumatic birth and bled so much she almost died, and another friend had her baby taken into intensive care after a really difficult labour. I already had a fear of childbirth, and all these accounts were just making it worse and worse. Of course, we only hear about the bad stories: thousands of women have an episiotomy (a small diagonal cut from the back of the vagina, to help the baby come out) and walk around absolutely fine, with healthy babies that otherwise might have been lost, but it's the horror stories that stayed in my head and really cemented my decision to never, ever have children.

Then another friend had her baby, and asked if I wanted to watch the video of it. I've never been into things like *One Born Every Minute*, the documentary series about women and their labours in a busy maternity ward, but suddenly I wanted to see this, and when I watched it, I cried my eyes out.

She was absolutely amazing. She was on her knees in a birthing pool, her partner in there too, and she was just making this really focused noise, like *Nnnnnnnn*, just working really hard and being a total warrior, until her baby came out and floated through her legs, then she watched it with this look on her face of total love, picked it up from the water and cradled it. The fact that I was bawling as I watched her, that's when I knew that I probably was ready to have a baby.

It was so beautiful. I mean, I'd be screaming like I was in *The Exorcist* and be thinking about all the possible complications if the baby were to become stuck and what condition my fanny was going to be in afterwards, but watching her made my admiration for any woman who even attempts the spontaneous birth route (where the baby is born through your tuppence, on the baby's schedule rather than the hospital's) shoot even higher. Some people might call me a coward for opting for an abdominal birth, but there's nothing cowardly about choosing to have major surgery where they cut through multiple layers of your abdomen, which comes with its own risks and involves an extremely painful recovery. For me, it was the least terrifying option for having my baby.

People often ask me why I call it an abdominal birth, rather than a C-section. Our amazing hypnobirthing doula, Emiliana, explained to us once that she liked to call it that because, 'A C-section sounds so medical. Plus, you're still giving birth. As far as I'm concerned, birth is birth, no matter how your baby arrives, and if you call it a C-section, the word birth isn't in there. And that's not fair because you're still giving birth to your baby.'

Other people don't look at it that way, but she holds firm that both abdominal births and spontaneous births are births. One of the things that had upset me about the thought of the C-section was exactly that; guilt that I was 'just' having an operation, a medical procedure that ended with us having a baby, which in fact was just science filling the gap between the other mammals giving birth and walking away fine, and all the women through history who had died because of blood loss or other complications when the medicine didn't exist to keep them alive. So to hear an experienced doula who had helped so many women with their births suggest that idea to us was amazing. Yeah, I *was* still giving birth – just out of my tummy.

THE FIRST TRIMESTER

I felt really shattered in that first trimester. I know it wasn't half as bad as some have had it – I know women who have been hospitalised with hyperemesis gravidarum, a type of extreme morning sickness that can involve prolonged vomiting, severe dehydration and dangerously low blood pressure – but I was shattered *all* the time. I felt like I'd been hit by a bus. I was so tired. On top of my sleep at night, I'd be having mid-morning naps until 1 p.m. and still feel knackered. It's crazy how your body just completely changes. You go from having infinite energy to being exhausted by everything: I'd get myself up, make a bowl of cereal, then need to sit down again for a rest. Unload the dishwasher, exhausted. If I took the dogs for a walk, I'd need a two-hour nap after. I wasn't sleeping a lot at night, and I permanently felt like I'd been out on a massive bender, without even the pleasure of a drink, a weekend in Ibiza, or any kind of wild nights out at all.

I felt so sick, too. Never vomited, but if I ate, I felt sick, if I didn't eat, I felt sick.

My other major symptom early on was that my boobs felt sore, which had always been usual for me just before my period, but my god, having an achy rack for months as they grew was tough, especially at night. They also got so veiny, with big green and blue veins making them like two giant road maps on my chest, and thanks to areola that had gone from normal size (whatever normal size is) to enormous saucer-sized, it was around that time that Boj came up with my new nickname: BIG DISCS! Lovely. I went for a run in week six – I say I went for a run, but I had to stop shortly after I started because I thought my nipples were bleeding. Running became a no-go very soon into my pregnancy because my nips were so sensitive it felt like someone was using a cheese grater on them. Brilliennnt.

And the veins didn't just stay on my boobs – I got new veins and broken capillaries on my legs, my bum, even my eyelids. I really panicked about the veiny eyelids, and ended up getting in touch with the doctor who had treated my varicose veins to say, 'WHAT IS HAPPENING TO ME?' He reassured me that it was all perfectly normal, even the thread veins that had popped up overnight all over my chest.

'They'll go,' he said (and they did).

I got this weird, corned beef skin all over my legs and bum, and I could not. Stop. Farting. For years I've never purposely guffed in front of Boj, but despite finding it highly embarrassing during pregnancy I had a serious case of windy pops. There was just no way of controlling them, and I was absolutely mortified. I'd get more and more embarrassed, and say, 'After seven years, I'm still not happy and comfortable with trumping in front of you. This isn't something I want to do.' He'd be laughing his head off, and tell me to accept it. Then I started burping too, I couldn't stop, and suddenly Boj realised he was living with my dad, hearing dad-burps and dad-trumps, for months on end. Thankfully it didn't put him off me.

These were the other highlights:

- Bleeding gums. It looked like a massacre every time I brushed my teeth
- Piles. Yep. Got a big bunch of bum grapes for Christmas. What a gift that was
- A stuffy nose! Throughout my entire pregnancy, I sounded so bunged up and dreamt of having clear nostrils again one day
- Fanny daggers. Or to put it more politely, lightning crotch. That's not fun, especially when it happens during a live radio show
- Leg cramps! Oh my god, I woke Boj up so many times when leg cramp would strike in the middle of the night, and later in the pregnancy, foot cramp. Cramp is so horrible, but for some reason I found it funny at the same time, a kind of tickly pain
- Cravings for vitamin C, so I wanted fresh orange juice and Capri Sun and McDonald's Still Fanta *all the time*; also fish finger sandwiches, at six weeks. That was the week Noa was called Captain Birdseye
- Baby brain:
  - ° I forgot Ant and Dec's names – I kept saying 'Who are those presenters, the double act, you know? PJ and Duncan!'

- ° I opened the fridge to look for a mop
- ° I had to google what 100cm was in metres.

But really I was lucky. I didn't get the thick hair I've always craved, that everyone said would come with pregnancy, but after the first trimester the nausea and tiredness went, my skin got better, and I loved seeing my bump grow. Although I couldn't run, I still felt fit, healthy and mobile, and only really struggled in the last few weeks when sleep became extremely uncomfortable, I couldn't see my tuppence because my bump was so ginormous and Boj had to tie my shoelaces for me. I'm so grateful that my body managed to keep me going throughout – I know so much of it is just luck, and people who do everything they can might still be knocked flat throughout their whole nine months. I remember being so happy and really looking forward to meeting Noa, and got so excited about being a mum that I genuinely thought: *I'm ready, I'm having a good pregnancy, this is all going to be easy.*

Little did I know exactly how much my body was lulling me into a false sense of security.

4

Baby Steps

It was around this point that things actually became proper, pregnancy-wise. It wasn't just positive tests and early symptoms – from this point onwards, I was well into hormones, scans, and names and (lockdown) baby showers.

THE FIRST SCAN

Besides Boj, the first person I told about my pregnancy was my best friend, Emma, who at the time lived in Connecticut in the States. I videocalled her from the bedroom of our flat and told her. She cried. I cried. It was amazing. But the second person I told was a young woman I'd never met before in my life. She was an osteopath and, before the session, needed to check if

I was pregnant, so I had to be transparent with her as she was about to go to work on my back. At the time (the pandemic) she was working from her parents' house, from a treatment room at the end of their garden, and after the session she called her mum outside and told her I was pregnant. Her mum fetched me a cup of herbal tea, sat me down in the warm sun of the garden, and started giving me lots of really good advice. It was so bizarre as I didn't know either of them, but there was this stranger, sharing her words of wisdom while I was desperately trying to make mental notes when I was still only two weeks preggo.

Otherwise, we didn't tell anyone until the twelve-week scan. I was aware of how common miscarriage is and how many of my friends had gone through it, and that my age made everything more risky. So nobody else knew.

Before the twelve-week scan, however, we had a private scan at ten weeks. I was aware that, as well as risk of miscarriage, my age meant a greater risk of Down's, Edwards' and Patau's – three syndromes that can affect children of later mothers. I knew health risks could go up with age, but I was shocked to discover that there's a 1 in 1500 chance when you're twenty, but by the time you're forty, it's 1 in 106. The NHS offers a CVS test, chorionic villus sampling, to pregnancies looking like they have a high probability of health issues, but the test involves a large needle being inserted into the placenta and carries a 1 in 100 risk of miscarriage, which is a difficult decision for any parent to make. I didn't know what we would do if the test found anything – it's impossible to say, really, unless it's actually happening to you, isn't it? – but I wanted to know so if it was a bridge we needed to cross, we'd at least know what was in front of us. On top of that, the twelve-week scan was at a time in the pandemic that meant Boj wouldn't be able to come with me for that or the twenty-week scan – the first time he would ever see our baby was after it was born, and I'd be alone for the NHS scans, seeing the teeny tiny foetus we'd both created, without Boj.

So we found a private clinic, which was still allowing partners to attend scans, offering a cell-free DNA blood test which was 99 per cent accurate for the three main syndromes, and which could tell us the sex too. It was a lot of money, but in a pregnancy so full of anxiety and at a time of COVID uncertainty, it was absolutely worth it for us. Fun fact, though: I discovered that if you have a baby, your baby's DNA will float around *your* body, in your blood and tissues, for *the rest of your life*. I don't know about you, but that blew my mind.

At the clinic, I was the most nervous I'd been throughout the pregnancy. I had that huge worry of,

What if our happy news suddenly turns to sad news? What if something's wrong, or there's no heartbeat? It was when we were sitting in the waiting room that I was so glad we'd decided to do this ten-week scan as I couldn't imagine being told any bad news without Boj. I was shaking as we walked into the doctor's office.

Once I was up on the bed, the doctor worked his magic and suddenly, on the mega TV by my feet, there was a little potato-shaped foetus, its heart beating away. It was so incredible. We both just stared at what we'd made. *We're having a baby.*

Then the image shifted, and we were looking at her in 3D. 'There you go!' the doctor said, 'Early 3D scan.'

'I didn't even know you could do that at 10 weeks!' I squealed.

'And how about the sex?' the doctor asked. 'Do you want to know?'

Boj said 'No' at the exact moment I said 'Yes'. He said he really wanted us to keep the sex of the baby as a surprise. I said, 'Listen, it's a surprise that I'm having this baby, OK? Tell you what – I'll find out, and I promise not to tell you. Then you can still have your surprise.' Funnily enough, he was happy to discover the sex after that. We had to wait a week for all the results, but it was peace of mind I really needed at that stage.

They called me a week later when I was at work, just about to go on air at Virgin Radio. They told me everything was OK with the baby, and I was absolutely over the moon. Then she said, 'Do you still want to know the sex?'

I was certain it was a boy. My twin sister has two boys, and my elder sister has two boys. I just knew I was having a boy too.

'It's a girl!' she said.

'Are you sure? Is that definite?'

'It's 99 per cent accurate,' she said. 'You're having a girl.'

I had been absolutely convinced it was a boy I was carrying. Now I had to go home and tell Boj. Of course, both of us just wanted a healthy, happy baby, but I don't think it's unusual for a woman to want a daughter and a man to want a son. There's no shame in that, is there? I think whatever people say, they have a preference one way or another, however much they end up loving any baby once it's born. My mum is so honest about how much she was disappointed with the fact that she had four grandsons and no granddaughters. Every time another one came along, she said, 'Another boy? I just want a granddaughter!' When my brother and his partner had a little girl, I felt like the pressure was off me a bit, so when I'd convinced myself I was having a boy,

I thought it was OK because my mum already had my niece.

That night I went home and said casually, 'By the way, I know what we're having. I got told before the show.'

'What?' Boj looked puzzled. 'Why didn't you call me?'

'Because it was ten to four and I was going on air and I wanted to tell you in person. So here we go.'

I had two Cornettos: a vanilla one in a blue wrapper, and a strawberry one in a red wrapper. 'I'm going to give you the one that matches the baby, OK? Blue for a boy, red for a girl. Ready? In fact, close your eyes.'

I put the red cone in his hand and waited for him to open his eyes. I thought he'd be so disappointed – I'd convinced him I was having a boy and he always wanted a son, and I felt bad for Boj. But he just said, 'I'm not disappointed! I'm really happy!' He was also staggered that I'd managed to keep it to myself for the entire afternoon and evening.

Once it sank in, we spoke about which football team she'd support.

'Obviously she's going to be an Arsenal fan,' I said.

'No way!' Boj argued. 'She's going to be Barnet through and through!'

'Our daughter is NOT wearing a Tango-orange football shirt on the weekends, Boj.'

Throughout the pregnancy, we often spoke about the

relationship I had with my dad, and I remember saying to Boj how much I hoped Noa's relationship with him would be the same. We also talked about who she'd look like or be like. I hoped she'd have Boj's brains, but not his massive head. Boj hoped she'd have my personality, but not my massive temper. There may be a natural instinct for parents to want their children to look like them, but I couldn't be more opposite – from the moment I fell pregnant I was hoping the baby would look like Boj, who was cute as a kid and is so handsome now. (I was walking with Noa the other day while she was wearing her pink woolly hat, and got chatting to an elderly man who asked, 'What a handsome baby – boy or girl?' Oh well, at least he thought Noa had her dad's good looks.)

By the time of the twelve-week scan, I wasn't nervous any more. I went alone to a cheerful but chaotic appointment – one nurse was shouting at a woman behind me for her poor social-distancing etiquette, two girls were arguing over who was first for their blood test, someone accidentally set the fire alarm off and nobody knew how to stop it, and my bladder wasn't full enough so the scan wasn't overly clear – but this scan too was positive news and we could breathe a sigh of relief. Our baby was healthy and we could finally share the news with our family and friends.

This is how it went with my parents:

Mum: What's this then? [looks at the scan photo on the front of a card, gasps] You're *lying*. Oh my god . . .

Dad: [finally puts on his glasses to look too]

Mum: No, you're *not*! No, it's not *you*. Who is it?

Dad: Well, it's got to be. Open it up.

Me: I'm having a baby.

Dad: [reads the message] Ah. Well done.

Mum: It's lovely. I'm getting emotional here!

Dad: [mimicking Mum's voice] *I'm getting emotional here.* Well. [takes off glasses, shrugs] Good luck to ya.

Mum: What about the wedding? Is this true? Are you having a laugh?

Me: It's true!

And with Boj's mum:

Sue: Is this true? You are not joking.

Boj: We're not joking!

Me: I'm three months pregnant.

Sue: [looks at the scan again] What is it?

Boj: It's a baby.

I don't know what it is about me and Boj, but every single person we told thought we were winding them up. Maybe that's what comes of spending your whole life saying you're definitely, 100 per cent, absolutely and positively never ever having a baby.

It was so emotional to finally tell people, and to talk about it on the *Maybe Baby* podcast not just as an idea we were debating, but about a reality we were facing. Now we were talking to people about what to expect, the challenges we might face and everything we could look forward to, so we discussed introducing the dogs to their new sister, helping them bond, and how they might feel, with the incredible Gemma Atkinson; the toxicity of pregnant women's trumps, the indignity of the label 'geriatric' for the over-forty mums, and the anxiety Anna Williamson experienced when she came off her medication with her first child; the loss of 50 per cent of our workforce when employers don't respect and protect their female employees, and the importance of keeping the chemistry going with your partner with Anna Whitehouse, aka Mother Pukka; and Boj even got to have a bit more dad preparation in our episode with Matt Willis, where we covered the shock of realising the baby you've discussed for ages with your partner is actually real, how parenting affects addiction, and how important the mantra 'it won't last' is for coping with children, whether you're facing something good or bad. This series wasn't just about our curiosity and trying to make a decision – it felt like we were doing real prep every time we talked about the nugget I was growing.

But one conversation in our off-mic life was really hard: telling one couple, some of our closest friends, about our pregnancy. The plan had always been for her and me to try and get pregnant at the same time and I was really excited at the prospect of us all becoming parents together because we lived so close to one another. At the time I fell pregnant, her job wasn't permanent, so out of caution they didn't want to start trying. She was a lot younger than me though, so obviously had time on her side, but that didn't help when we broke the news. She started crying, and although they were tears of joy, I could tell she was upset and my heart was breaking for her. They were both congratulating us but trying to hold back their own sadness that we were no longer going to be new parents at the same time, and I felt terribly guilty.

Another one of my best friends in the whole world had been trying for years to get pregnant, and on top of that she'd had unsuccessful IVF treatment more than once, as well as a miscarriage, so I couldn't face sharing my pregnancy news the traditional way our group of girls announced it, over a dinner in front of everyone.

I texted her the news, so she'd have space to react however she wanted, without me watching her. She said she
was really happy for me.

I met her for lunch the following week. She passed
me a card that said: Congratulations, You're Pregnant.
Inside, she'd written: *You're not the only one!* She was due
two weeks after me. I couldn't believe it. After all this,
we'd be doing it together, when she'd been wanting a
baby for so long! One of my oldest, best friends was
pregnant, and it honestly was the best feeling ever.

Then, at her twelve-week scan, they discovered her
baby had a gap at the base of the spine and issues with
the formation of the stomach, was incompatible with
life and wouldn't have survived longer than a week if
she had gone full term. She had to have a termination.
It was devastating. We had all been so happy, so happy
for her, it had been such a long time, and this was the
furthest she'd ever got in a pregnancy. I couldn't believe
it had happened to her. When was she ever going to get
a break? I lay in bed and cried for a week thinking of her
loss. We all grieved with her.

That pain never goes away, for the mothers and fa-
thers who lose a baby at any stage. But a few months
later, they decided to start IVF again and this time
did genetic testing on a whole fresh round of embryos,
spent the next nine months having extra scans and extra

care with a new pregnancy, and a beautiful big bump. And in October 2021 she and her husband finally met their perfect, beautiful little boy after a complication-free, planned abdominal birth. There are no words to describe their joy.

THE THIRD TRIMESTER

When the third trimester rolled around, the fun really started and I fully lost my mind. It began all right: at thirty weeks I had a really good video call with my NHS obstetrician about birth options, and we discussed my fear of childbirth along with various facts and figures on both abdominal and spontaneous births. She was, thankfully, very understanding and told me that with elective abdominal births on the NHS, they'd book me in for my due date minus seven days, which made it 15 February, the day after Valentine's Day. Knowing I could have my baby the way I wanted to made the final trimester feel like it would be much more enjoyable. The idea of major surgery didn't exactly excite me, but I felt it was a better option than a baby head-butting its way out of my tuppence. It made me less anxious and more at ease, knowing that was how our little girl would be born, and I still wish everyone could choose, ask for, and receive exactly the birth that suits them best. I know that's a huge issue – too many women are ignored or bullied into births that leave them traumatised or physically injured, and there are countless amazing women campaigning to improve that.

After a blissful second trimester, where I felt great and looked glowing, those last three months turned me into an emotional wreck, crying a lot, and my bump had got to the stage where I wasn't able to sleep because I was so uncomfortable, looking like I'd swallowed a beach ball with a wriggling octopus inside. I was in full nesting mode, too, which caused massive tension between me and Boj because he kept accusing me of shifting his stuff around and sometimes throwing it in the bin. Not true.

OK, maybe once. Or twice.

(He caught me cleaning at midnight, too.)

With that animalistic nesting instinct, I wanted the house completely done, with everything in its place for when the baby arrived. I was like a woman possessed, and finally understood what those women had been talking about on our podcast when they thanked their partners for putting up with their crazy pregnancy hormones. For instance:

- I cried when InstaStories uploaded in the wrong order for an ad campaign.

- I cried because Boj said I'd moved our thermostat when I hadn't.
- I cried because I couldn't find my favourite room spray, which the painters accidentally threw out.

And when I wasn't crying, I was just being an absolute arsehole to Boj, while the baby tapdanced on my bladder. My hormones were obviously much more of a stress to him, because to me, it was just another part of pregnancy to roll with, but to him, being patient and supportive, he'd get these blasts of negativity and just not be able to do anything. Occasionally I'd kind of come to, and think, *Christ, I'm surprised he's still here. I will be completely surprised if he's still around by the time I have this baby*. I just felt like I was losing the plot. Crazy.

And that can be super scary, to feel like you're being a total arsehole and pushing away the people who are caring for you the most. I never thought I'd experience a pregnancy and now it was happening, I spent every day worrying about whether she'd be born a healthy baby. At every scan I was petrified there would be no heartbeat, and every time I went to the toilet, I was afraid of seeing blood. I didn't know if it was 'normal' to be worrying so much – all I could think about was the bond I'd already formed with her, and how we would deal with any bad news that might come. It was my biggest fear.

One of the things that helped was a mindful birthing course I did, with hypnobirthing doula Emiliana. I think that fear of childbirth was behind a lot of my behaviour during the pregnancy, all the worries coming out as bad moods, and the course helped me overcome a lot of those fears and gave me a tonne of information about the process of childbirth and what happens in spontaneous and abdominal births, plus calming techniques that turned out to be invaluable. It meant that when I went for my thirty-two-week scan, to check growth and whether my placenta had moved from its riskier, low-lying position at the previous twenty-week scan, I wasn't freaking out and could take in the news that everything was fine without fist-pumping the air and running around the wards.

We're so lucky to be in a country where women can ask for a selective C-section, or a home birth, a hospital birth, a midwife-led birth. Obviously it depends on availability on the day, and the circumstances around your labour, but it's really nice that you can choose the birth you want, particularly if you have a fear of childbirth or hospitals. I'd recommend having as many informed conversations as you can with experts in birth to find out the pros and cons, and to think carefully about what you'd like. The photos and videos I've seen now make me almost wish I could have a water birth or home birth, because they look so calm and peaceful, but I know at the time I wanted to be near *all* the doctors and drugs and knives if anything went wrong. What was I going to do if the baby got stuck and we were at our house? Hand Boj some tools to get it out? Ask Baxter and Shirley to call 999?

For that reason, it's also really good to make a birth plan before the baby comes, but to think of it as birth preferences, rather than a fixed plan. If things change or don't go as expected around your due date, it may cause worry, fear or disappointment when having to change your fixed plan. I felt far less pressure having birth *preferences* which I knew may not be a given or could be adapted at any time. I was so pleased that I had my preferences written down, then when my waters broke three days early, I knew I could still have a birth I wanted, because I'd been really well prepared for what could happen. Having preferences and getting it all written down makes you think everything through and prepare, and it's quite exciting too: making a playlist, asking for dimmer lights (because your body tenses up lying down on your back, legs open under bright lights with strangers all around you – as Siobhan, our night nanny, says, you wouldn't want to make the baby that way, so why would you want it born like that?), making things feel more familiar and relaxed. The mindful birthing course we did was great for helping us get ready, and letting us know what would happen, step by step, rather than us having to ask continual questions on the day and not know what was 'normal' and what needed more support from Boj or the medical team. You can't do much about the specific labour, but if you're informed you can make better choices around how to make it easier for yourself, by knowing what should happen around you and having elements you can control: music, smells, clothes or blankets, who's with you (and who's not), things like that. One of my friends opted to not have any kind of plan at all, just to go with the flow, but her whole experience ended up being far more complicated and negative because she didn't know what she could or should be asking for. Planning helps you prepare for all the things that may happen, not just the stuff you want.

A VERY COVID PREGNANCY

Being pregnant during the COVID-19 pandemic had its ups and downs. I fell pregnant right at the end of May 2020, when Virgin Radio were still allowing presenters to do shows from our studios in town. It was strange to walk through an eerily quiet City area of London on my Monday-to-Friday commute, but those days were also bright and sunny, and gave me a chance to be outside during lockdown.

The downsides were that some of my best friends never saw me pregnant at all; even my siblings only saw me a couple of times. On the other hand, I thought not being able to have any big nights out would leave me with massive FOMO, but because of the pandemic, there were no weddings, birthdays, festivals or parties happening for anyone. In a very selfish way, at least I wasn't actually missing out . . .

We'd been told a while before my due date that Boj might not be able to be with me at the birth. That was upsetting, and my heart goes out to every woman who's faced childbirth without their chosen birth partner, at any time. Our focus was always just on getting to meet a healthy, happy baby, and the fact that the timing of her arrival coincided with a change in policy that meant Boj was allowed to join me was just the icing on the cake.

COVID also meant I couldn't have a massive baby shower, which was a relief – I'm not one for huge events where everyone's looking at me and making a fuss. But I did say I wanted to do a gender reveal for my family, because I knew my mum and sisters really cared about that kind of stuff. Boj said, 'Isn't it a bit over the top? Do we have to do a gender reveal?'

Boj was clearly thinking of those couples in America who end up burning down their own house because they've attempted some ridiculous stunt, so I had to explain we were just going to burst a balloon or cut a cake or something. That's all. We weren't about to have a plane flying over dropping pink or blue clouds of smoke over the neighbourhood and causing some minor local disaster. I promised him that no one was going to die.

I asked my parents if we could have an afternoon in their garden to tell them the baby's sex, if they wanted, but I didn't want any fuss and they didn't have to do anything. I'd be bringing a balloon (which had pink confetti inside) and by August 2020 we were allowed to meet in groups of twenty outside, so we could invite my siblings, and their partners and children. I kept saying to Mum, 'Don't do anything! You don't have to organise anything special!' But on the bank holiday we'd arranged it for, I came back to theirs after collecting the balloon and found my mum had filled the dining room with a massive buffet and some decorations – even for me this was a little extra, but *nice*, not balloon-arch-and-full-floral-arrangement-in-the-garden extra, which isn't my thing. It was such a good family party, after we'd not seen each other for all those months, and when we popped the balloon everyone went crazy. I mean, whatever the sex everyone would have gone crazy, because it's one of those moments, isn't it, but my sister-in-law and brother were extra excited to be having another girl in the family.

I also did a little reveal on Instagram, involving the doggies, of course – along with a single pair of pink baby booties – and had two surprise mini-showers via Zoom which were so special that I didn't feel like I missed out. If anything, it might be just how I would have chosen it.

BABY NAMES

We knew we were calling her Noa from so early on. If she'd been a boy, I had a list of boys names: Caleb, Ezra, Isaac, Jessie and Zach. I'd say them to myself to try them out: 'Zach Bojtos, Seth Bojtos. Jesse Bojtos.' I really liked Ezra, but Boj wasn't a fan. As a girl's name, I also liked Millie – specifically Millie Bobbie Bojtos, but that got shut down fairly swiftly too, and when we looked at her for the first time, we knew she wasn't a Millie.

Both our mums were suggesting names from the very first day they knew I was pregnant. My mum sent me a list of boys and girls names that very evening – in fact, she also sent it to Boj, clearly hoping with a pincer movement one of the names would get chosen, and I discovered later she had also sent it to my brother and his partner for their baby the year before, when they too decided none of the names were for them. They really surprised me: Kourtney, Kendall, Kylie – stop trying to name my baby after a bloody Kardashian, Mum! Anastasia too, oddly. Who knows where that came from? Maybe she's a fan.

Boj's mum, Sue, asked that, if it was a girl, would we give her Boj's grandma's name: Ilse. Boj was really close to his grandma Ilse, and he didn't know any of his grandparents apart from her. She survived the Holocaust, was liberated from Auschwitz at the end of the war – although the rest of her family died there – and went on to marry Sue's dad, who had also lost all of his family at Auschwitz. She was an utterly remarkable woman with so many stories, eventually dying at the age of seventy-nine on Boj's twelfth birthday, so it made sense that Sue would ask us to think of her mother's name.

Boj said, 'Mum! You can't put us on the spot like that.'

When we told her that if it was a girl, we were going to call her Noa, the room went silent. Sue nodded, then said, 'What about Hannah? Or Helena?' I had the funniest feeling she wasn't that keen on our name. We'd really struggled to come up with girls' names, then Boj reminded me how much I liked his cousin's wife's name, one that apparently was very popular in Israel. Perfect. Noa.

But Sue said, 'No, no, you can't call her Noa because it's bad luck in Jewish tradition to call a baby the name of somebody that you know who isn't dead.' We were really gutted, because we thought we'd found the perfect name and now Sue had told us it was impossible. Fortunately, Boj reminded his mum that not only was the daughter of her very-much-alive best friend named after her, but that Sue had also named her daughter after her living best friend.

'Are you basically trying to get us to call the baby Ilse because you don't want Noa?' I asked.

'No, it's bad luck!' she insisted.

'No Sue,' we said, 'we'll be fine.' So Noa it was.

We couldn't just stick with Noa Ilse Bojtos, though, as I didn't fancy her being NIB through her life, so we added Daisy (one of my mum's suggestions!) as I really liked the name. We've already had about a hundred people say, 'Isn't Noah a boy's name?' and stick the H on there. Mum still insists she's called Noa-Daisy, as a way to emphasise her role in name selection, I suppose, which is very sweet but I constantly remind her there's no hyphen and Daisy is just her middle name. I'm sure she'll get it one day. We also thought we needed something a bit easier in there because Bojtos, a Hungarian name, isn't the most obvious of surnames to pronounce. Most people say it 'Bodge-toss', hence Boj's nickname, but it's actually 'Boy-tosh'. So now she's got a first name everyone thinks is male, and a surname no one can pronounce. *Brilliennnnnt.*

We called her Noa throughout most of the pregnancy, with Nugget and Nutchky as nicknames, then Potato after she was born (because of a meme we saw which said 'let the potato rest for five minutes' and whenever she was napping we started saying 'The Potato is resting'), which gradually shortened to Tayto. Other nicknames for our beautiful daughter included MC Grindah, after the Kurupt FM CEO in *People Just Do Nothing* with a combed forward fringe, and Alan Brazil, the Scottish footballer and broadcaster who has a big red face, who Noa had a look of when straining for a poo. I still find it so bizarre when parents get to the birth of their child and still don't know what to call them. Surely if you have nine months to come up with a name, you can decide on one by the time the baby is born? Nine months guys! One of my friends went two weeks post-birth without naming her baby. I guess sometimes when the baby comes out, they just don't look right for their name. And I know that's possible, because my little brother was called Sam for the first two weeks of his life and my parents were even sent cards which had 'Congratulations on the birth of baby Sam' inside. Then Mum decided he didn't look like a Sam and changed his name to Robert instead. Thankfully, Noa looked like a Noa from the first moment we saw her.

A word with . . . Emiliana
(our hypnobirthing doula)

I met Kate when she signed up for my private
hypnobirthing course for abdominal birth (rather
than physiological, or vaginal birth). Usually
hypnobirthing courses are for physiological birth,
but having had both types of births, I recognised
there was a need for emotional support and education around an abdominal birth too – I teach the
courses separately, according to the mum's birth
choice, but actually both are completely inter-
twined, because a vaginal birth can become an
emergency C-section, and a planned abdominal
birth can go into spontaneous labour early.

The aim of the courses is to give mums the
tools and techniques of mindfulness to navigate
the unexpected turns of birth, particularly when
you're doing it for the first time. There's no kind of
'normal birth', and having that information about
the options you have – at each stage of the labour,
where you want to give birth, what happens on
the day – will all help you to relax, to enjoy it
rather than to feel scared. I knew Kate was scared

about her birth, but she was so open to learning and to finding a way to overcome her fears.

The affirmations that Kate found so helpful are all about rewiring the brain and helping the mind–body connection, so instead of feeling panic because your mind thinks that you're in danger, practising the idea that birth is positive: maybe it's about imagining holding your baby in your arms, or using breathing techniques to ride the waves your body is feeling and fill your body with oxygen to counter the fight or flight instincts. Even in general life, those exercises can be so helpful, to bring us back to a calm, relaxed state when our adrenaline is peaking, and in birth, using visualisation to reduce that panic, to imagine what your baby might feel like, look like, smell like: this can be so helpful in making your body feel positive and calm.

Post-birth, different doulas do different things for the mums and the families, but my main role is being there for the mum to talk to, to debrief the birth, even if it feels like it was very straight-forward, and helping her with the healing process if it's been more complicated. Sometimes looking after the mum means looking after the baby, but sometimes it's just about nurturing the mum and helping her be in a peaceful environment with a cup of tea. People should hire the doula according to what they think they'll need: some people wouldn't like the thought of someone else tidying their house, others know that's exactly what would help them, so it's important you click with a doula before hiring them. It's totally normal for a house to be chaotic after the birth of a baby and for the parents to look sleep deprived – I'd be a bit worried if I came to a house that was sparkling clean with everyone smiley and dressed!

As a doula, I don't give any medical advice, but I do offer signposting to help mums get the most up-to-date, unbiased information so they can decide what's best for them. Being a doula is the best job. You get to support the parents emotionally and just be there for them, and that's worth so much. My hypnobirthing courses start at £10 because I want the tools and techniques to be accessible, particularly when partners can't always be at the midwife appointments.

If you're thinking about becoming a parent, my

top advice would be: don't look at other people's pregnancy or birth stories with the idea of comparing yours with theirs. Prioritise investing in support over equipment, and focus on your own journey, because it's so special, and will always be completely unique to you.

5

Labour and Pain

I'd put so much effort into trying to relax about the whole thing that when the time for labour actually rolled around, I was only bothering to finish work a week before my planned birth date. Boj suggested that maybe I should do myself a favour and take two weeks before the baby came, but I always, always want to squeeze everything into the smallest possible period of time to see if I can just about get away with things.

'I'll be fine! I'll be fine – a week is enough.' He kept on persisting and in the end I decided my last radio show would be two weeks before Noa's arrival.

Then on 11 February, four days before my scheduled abdominal birth, I woke up at 5.45 a.m. with a sharp pain across my tummy and the discovery that I'd wet the bed. I felt trickles of water down my leg, and got out my phone torch to get a better look. *Oh shit.* For some reason I just thought my pelvic floor had given way, so went and sat on the toilet for a while, but nothing happened so I got back into bed.

I'd heard from everyone that the first baby is always late, so reassured myself that 'just' wetting myself was another pregnancy symptom, but as soon as I lay down: more water began leaking out. At that point I woke up Boj.

'Boj. I think my waters have broken.'

He was fast asleep.

'BOJ! My waters are breaking!'

Eventually he woke up, slightly, and said, 'No they aren't.'

'I've just wet myself. Twice. And look!' I shone the torch onto the bedsheets. Pink.

This is it.

Boj immediately wanted to check I wasn't being dramatic and googled 'are my waters breaking?' . . . he was half asleep.

Once he'd fully woken up, we called the hospital, and the nurse said, 'Yup, that sounds like your waters.' I burst into tears – this wasn't the plan! Suddenly, I wasn't in control, after months of organising and talking to my GP, various obstetricians, my midwife and booking in the surgery. She reassured me, saying, 'It's OK, you can still have the birth you want, just calm down, and come in and see us in the next couple of hours.'

We really took our time. We made breakfast, I re-packed my hospital bag, Boj had a shower, I had a shower, and we phoned our friend who was supposed to have Baxter and Shirley for the single day that I was meant to be in hospital. By that stage, I wasn't leaking any more and there were no further signs I was in labour. We got a taxi down to the Whittington, where Boj had to wait outside the maternity ward in the corridor because of the pandemic, and I was taken in and strapped up to a contraction-tracking machine, measuring the length and frequency of my contractions, where I had to press a handheld button every time I felt something. *Why* did I go into labour eleven days before my due date? Boj and I still don't quite agree on this. I believe it was because the previous day we'd taken the dogs somewhere we'd not walked before and I was vigorously marching up the most enormous hill, breathing out of my arse. Boj, on the other hand, is convinced it was my cooking, as I'd made the driest, most disgusting chestnut and quorn-chicken pie. He believes Noa couldn't bear any more of my cooking, even filtered through my placenta.

When the obstetrician came, she began to ask me why I was having a C-section. I felt really uncomfortable as she went on to explain how busy they were, how many planned births they had booked in, would I definitely not be prepared to at least consider a vaginal birth?

'But . . . I'm having a C-section, it's been planned for ages . . . I've spoken to my doctor . . .' I could feel myself spiralling as the obstetrician came and went over several hours, continually trying to convince me to give birth in the way that terrified me most. It felt like they'd just arrived and said out of the blue, 'Can you just change your mind quickly, this thing you've thought about for ages?' That's what it felt like, an issue that I'd agonised over again and again, and here I was at a crucial point, being judged, criticised and pressured to go back on what we'd thought about so much.

The next thing I knew, I was calling Boj, sobbing, and he marched into the ward and confronted the first person he saw. I don't know exactly what Boj said to them, but a lovely Irish midwife came to find me in the toilet where I was crying my eyes out.

'Are you OK?'

I wiped my face down, puffy-eyed and make-up everywhere. 'Yeah, I'm fine.'

She gave me a look. 'What's wrong?'

I told her what had happened with the obstetrician, and she smiled at me, and said, 'Don't worry, you're having the birth you want today. We're going to get you up to the pre-labour ward, and you *will* have the birth you want. Do not panic.'

The contrast between her and the obstetrician was huge. If you don't have that fear of childbirth – tokophobia, it's called – I think it's almost impossible to understand how crippling it can be, and how to speak to somebody that has it. I was shaking when I was told I might not have a C-section, knowing that I'd never have got pregnant in the first place if I hadn't had the surgical option. I'd spoken to my GP before we were even trying, and asked whether I could have an elective C-section.

'Yes,' she said. 'In this country, you can. In other countries, it's not an option – only in medical emergencies. But here, that's fine.' I don't think I ever would have had a child if a spontaneous birth was my only way. Both options, honestly, were frightening, but it's really important that women have a choice, even for non-medical reasons, and that they can talk to their midwife or doctor to understand the benefits and risks of each kind of birth. Talking to Mary, the lovely midwife, was one of those moments where I realised how important it is to have someone speaking up for you at your birth – whether it's a birthing partner, a doula, or an understanding and empathetic medical professional. I can see how so many women end up having damaging births, because at that moment you don't have the expertise or the authority to stand up to professionals saying you *have* to do it their way.

When I was told it would be OK and I was being taken in, I felt the biggest relief ever. Other than the time I was crying when Mary found me, I was so calm on the day. Upstairs at the hospital, we were taking photos of me getting ready to have our baby, getting into my very sexy dark green compression stockings and my hospital gown, calling my mum to say the baby was coming early. We were also doing a bit of filming for the *Celebrity Bumps* MTV show; they'd given us a camera and a tripod and we used it to film the birth (from the head end, obviously) – it's so amazing to watch that back now. I watch that over and over again, and I hope Noa might want to see it one day.

Thanks to the hypnobirthing we'd done with our amazing doula, Emiliana, I felt totally calm and in control, repeating the words from the affirmation cards even as my contractions grew stronger. Emiliana had hosted a hypnobirthing course specifically for abdominal birth, which meant that when we went into the pre-labour ward I was totally ready for when the operation would be, how long it would take, exactly what would happen at each stage. I know that really we can't control things like birth, but knowing exactly what was about to happen made me feel so much more prepared, and I really recommend something like this for anyone going

for an abdominal birth, especially those with tokophobia. We'd spoken about the different choices we could
make – dimmed lights, your own music playlist – which
added to everything feeling really calm as the surgical
team introduced themselves to us one by one. (I dread
to think what state Boj would have been in if he'd had
to watch me give birth like a panicking wild animal.)

For some reason, I'd made a playlist that was about
six hours long, when we'd only be in theatre for around
forty-five minutes, so we put it on shuffle apart from
when the doctor said Noa was about to be born, and
I remember songs from London Grammar, Massive
Attack, Jose Gonzalez, Jack Garratt and Michael Kiwa-
nuka playing, loads of really lovely, chilled out sounds,
which I suppose a lot of people have with their births.
I can't imagine too much drum and bass gets played
in theatre. Then when it was time, Boj put on 'I Love
You Always Forever' by Donna Lewis, and they lifted
Noa out.

What was really lovely was that I didn't feel a ruddy
thing, pain-wise. Pre-surgery, as the spinal block went
in, I had to stay so still, and then I gradually went completely numb. I was lying down on the bed trying to
lift my legs, and the anaesthetist said, 'OK, lift your
leg.' And when I tried – nothing. Dead. He was using
a cold spray on various parts of my body saying, 'Let

me know when it's *as* cold as it was when I sprayed it on your shoulder. Let me know when it's as cold.' You could have punched me and I wouldn't have felt a thing. In theatre, Boj was a fantastic birthing partner, stroking my head and keeping me calm, and I had just a vague sense of the doctors moving something around inside me; it was only when they said, 'Kate, she's going to be here in a matter of seconds,' that I really got this feeling of pushing and pulling, like they were forcing something right up to my sternum. The cut is only about four to six inches long and babies are generally a lot bigger than that; it's so small comparatively, so they really have to pull to get the baby out.

And then she was there! I love the time and date she was born: 11.02.2021 at 2:01 p.m. As one of the lovely ladies placed Noa on to me for our first skin-to-skin contact she said two words: 'One daughter'. Boj and I both began to cry – and Boj *never* cries – and they asked if Boj wanted to cut the cord, and he said, 'No, thank you, not for me, you can do that. It's just tokenism, isn't it? I'm not actually useful here, you get to do all the proper stuff, I'll see her when she's back.' So they took her away to be checked over, which is necessary in a C-section, and whisked her back before I could even notice. It had been the most calm, magical birth I could have imagined.

When they put her back on me, they sewed me up, which felt like it took longer than the actual surgery but the whole thing was a matter of minutes. I realised that the surgical drapes were so far up my body that, to fit Noa on me for skin-to-skin contact, she was balanced at the very edge of my collar bone, a little scarf baby, and I couldn't see her face.

'Boj! I can't see her! What does she look like!'

Boj looked at our precious, beloved, newborn daughter for a moment. 'She looks like she's been involved in a fight with Anthony Joshua.' She was a teeny tiny squished up mess, but who wouldn't be if they'd been curled up in a tiny ball for nine months then physically wrenched into the world by a pair of giant hands?

As soon as I was sewn up, we were taken to the post-theatre ward, the recovery room, to wait for about an hour. Being wheeled out of theatre, I don't think we needed anything but the three of us. We were so high and euphoric, just in awe of what we'd made, and sharing this precious moment with Boj – who was taking a million photos – felt totally magical. Noa got onto my boob and started feeding, and I immediately fell in love. It was amazing, a rush of emotions and oxytocin running through my body, listening to Noa feeding and her sweet little lamb-like sounds; we were completely in awe and in love. A midwife came over and watched us for a while. Then she came a little closer, and watched a little more.

'I'm not sure I like those noises she's making,' she said.

'What do you mean?'

'It sounds like she's singing,' she said, so I looked down and all I saw was a normal, healthy baby, feeding. 'That's not always a good thing. I'm just going to get a second opinion.'

She brought over another doctor, and they observed Noa feeding then had a conversation between themselves, then came over to us. 'Right. Basically, when a baby is not pushed through the vaginal canal, it's possible for fluid to still remain in their lungs. When we take them out of the tummy, their lungs haven't always been completely drained, which is dangerous as they can have difficulty breathing properly,' It was only half an hour since Noa was born.

'We're going to need to take her to intensive care because it could be water on the lungs, or it could be an infection. We have to take her to NICU, the Newborn Intensive Care Unit.'

I couldn't even speak. I'd chosen the C-section because it was all planned and nothing could go wrong. But then this happened and all I could think of was: *Oh God, my baby.*

They brought round the incubator, and put her in

there, hooked up to the tubes. I asked Boj to go with her so she wasn't alone, I couldn't bear the thought of our Noa being anywhere on her own when she'd only just left my body, the place she'd been safe for nine months, and was now heading up to a distant hospital wing in a plastic trolley. So he left, and then I was suddenly, for the first time in months, completely and horribly on my own.

We went from feelings of joy, happiness, gratitude, and euphoria, to feeling confused and scared. I'll never forget going up to the post-natal ward, surrounded by women with their babies, while my baby was nowhere near me. All I could do was pray that Noa would be OK.

6

Post-natal

I'd asked Boj to go with her. But then I was left on my own and I was so frightened. I was messaging my parents and my best friends, saying, 'She's gone to NICU, I don't know when she's coming back.' In the post-natal ward I couldn't even get out of bed, and eventually when he came to the ward I suggested Boj go home. 'She's in intensive care, I'm fine, once my catheter's out I can visit her. You go and get washed, get some rest.' There was no point in him trying to stay in the world's most uncomfortable chair on the post-natal ward. As soon as he left, I tried to get up to see if I was ready to have my catheter out, and immediately threw up. Clearly not ready yet. After a short nap, all the feeling was back in my body, my catheter was removed, and the nurse accompanied me to the bathroom to help me have a wash.

'Let's take you up to NICU, shall we?'

In the NICU, I was allowed to pick Noa up and put her on me, and the nurse offered to call me every time Noa needed feeding, so I spent the first twenty-four hours on call, going back and forth. I loved going to see her there, watching her and sitting by her incubator, breast-feeding her in my nightie. I was looking at photos of her recently and can't believe how tiny she was as we sat there in the dark, listening to the beeping of the other machines and the whisperings of the nurses. The only lights were on the equipment, and even though it's ultimately a scary place to be as a new parent, there was something very comforting about being there with her, knowing I could feed and nourish her, and was actually doing a proper job of caring for her, along with the fantastic team of doctors and nurses.

The next day, Noa was moved into the Neo Natal Unit, which meant she was out of the greatest danger, and she was also now on the same floor as my ward. I was still spending all of my time walking very slowly through the cold, quiet corridors of the hospital, back and forth, feeding her, watching her, and they were giving her tiny little IV drips. They tried to take her off the oxygen, but her signs and vitals weren't right so she stayed on them for another long twenty-four hours.

Life on the post-natal ward, meanwhile, was not so great. Not only could I hear new parents with their babies, I was right next to a woman who spent her entire time eavesdropping on any conversation I had with Boj, even though the unspoken rule on a ward is that if the curtains are drawn, you always pretend you can't hear anything over the machines and trolleys. Boj and I would be talking quietly to each other and we'd suddenly hear her chime in. We tried to see the funny side as she sounded just like Shirley from *Eastenders*.

'You been to see your baby yet? Did you have a C-section? Still haven't got her with you? What happened? The food's rubbish in here, isn't it?'

Boj and I would look at each other, roll our eyes and I'd answer her questions without trying to start a full-on conversation, but she was such a busybody. All I wanted to do was speak to Boj in private about Noa's progress and what the doctors had told me, but it felt like we were having a three-way conversation.

Just as we were beginning to make plans to go home, packing our bags and getting ourselves ready, they stopped us. 'I'm sorry, Noa's lost too much weight in intensive care.' When they saw our faces, they said, 'You can go home with her now, but you'll have to have a visit from the midwife tomorrow. And if she hasn't put on enough weight in twenty-four hours, you'll have to both come back in, but you won't be able to come back to this ward – you'll have to come through A&E. It's up to you.'

I looked at Boj, and at Noa, and said, 'I'll stay here.'

By this point, I'd been moved to a room where I could get some sleep, seeing as I didn't have Noa with me, and it was great. If it looks like you might be in hospital for a while, or if you aren't able to be with your baby, I really recommend asking if they have any private rooms you can stay in, rather than in the wards just separated by a thin curtain from eleven other women, crisp packets opening, dads snoring, babies crying. Sometimes if they have availability they won't charge you, but you may end up paying a small fee, which I'm sure varies between hospitals, and you can keep asking if any have become free at any time you're in there. I'm so grateful that Kelly, one of the lovely midwives at the Whittington, moved me from the ward to my own room for some peace and privacy for a couple of nights. It made a big difference in terms of recovery and bonding. Boj came in with M&S food, homemade porridge, a fried egg roll and a fresh coffee, and we sat with Noa, taking loads of photos of us with her just in a little nappy because hospital rooms are so warm and toasty. We knew she was going to be fine. I stayed up all night breastfeeding, getting tips on holds and latches from the midwives, how to swaddle and care for her. It was just like in Mum's day. In the hospital bed, Noa's cot was exactly the same height as my pillow, and I'd watch her through this happy haze of tiredness and medication, still feeling out of it, but really enjoying it too.

The next day she still hadn't put on quite enough weight, but they said we could possibly go home, under the same conditions as before: she would be weighed at ours in another twenty-four hours, and if it hadn't gone up sufficiently, back we'd come.

But I was determined. I said to Boj, 'I know that I can do this. I can just feed her feed her feed her, and by tomorrow, I know she'll have put on enough. It's been five days now. I just want to go home, sleep in my own bed and see the doggies.'

As we left the Whittington and I watched Boj carrying Noa in the car seat, I had a sudden terror. How were they letting us leave? We didn't know what the hell we were doing! It was so surreal – how we were going anywhere with a *baby*? – and the first time I'd had fresh air in five days. I remember Boj driving home at twelve miles an hour; how we didn't get stopped by the police I'll never know. I was sitting in the back saying, 'Slow down! Boj, slow down!' the entire way back. She lay in her seat as Boj went even slower over the bumps, not making a sound, sleeping through it all.

At home, we ordered vegan burgers and fries, and

watched her go to sleep, our last night before we got Shirley and Baxter home the next day to introduce them to Noa. It's great if you have pets or older children to be able to send them somewhere nice for a night, that they'll enjoy and feel safe, so you can have a settling-in period, then welcome them back and introduce them in a calm, relaxed home once you've washed and got yourself a little bit settled. I asked Boj where the Michelin-star meal was that we'd ordered for Valentine's Day, to cook at home before going in for the birth, and he confessed that he'd eaten it back here all on his own, all three courses, both of ours at once. What a sad little meal. But I didn't care; we were on cloud nine, and we couldn't stop kissing her and kissing each other, sniffing the top of her little head. There's a video I remember taking of her, where she's sitting on my lap in a navy floral babygro with a little frilly collar, just going *hic, hic, hic*, looking around like an animal, like a little bird. I was so in love and so besotted and obsessed already, I felt like there would be no issue in me bonding with her, something I'd heard and worried about. I was completely in love. Then, that night I woke up in the middle of the night absolutely convinced that she was dead. You know in movies, you see people gasp and sit bolt upright, and you think, *Shut up, that doesn't happen?* Well, I did that. Which wasn't a great idea after abdominal surgery. It was excruciatingly painful, and I couldn't stop crying, thinking I'd opened the wound.

Those first twenty-four hours at home, I breastfed her like *mad*, and when the midwife came Noa was finally a safe weight. I was so pleased to be back at home, back at last, with Noa and Boj and Baxter and Shirley – who, by the way, had gone to one of our best friend's house the day I went to hospital and ended up staying with them for five days, and we'd missed each other massively. I thought, *Great, that's the end of all the drama, we're all back together and can finally relax and start our lives as a pack of five.* The first few days at home were actually pretty good: my milk supply had come in and I was still quite high, and really excited that Noa was here.

I mean, it was tiring too, and overwhelming, knowing that our lives were never going to be the same again. We had the health visitor constantly coming to check on Noa, but we also had our doula, Emiliana, doing a couple of days for us as well. She'd come and answer a million questions we had for her, show us how to use the sling and put Noa in it, make us tea, do some cleaning and helping around the house. Obviously there was family that wanted to visit, but they couldn't because of COVID. A lot of my friends were saying, 'That's great, you don't want anyone coming over in the first few days. It can be just you guys! You can just be in your bubble!'

But I was desperate to see people – it was hard enough during my pregnancy when we couldn't visit family or friends, and that was before sleep deprivation kicked in and I needed my loved ones who could help and comfort me. Everyone should understand though, that the mum and baby are the priority after birth – everyone wants to come and meet the baby, but there should be no pressure on anyone at that stage, no guilt-trips about what you ought to be doing for the sake of other people. Not least because the baby's immune system is nowhere near ready for them to be surrounded by tons of people, even when we aren't in a pandemic. In the first few weeks, their immunity is growing daily, but young babies have still been lost due to infections unintentionally passed on by unknowing visitors. They aren't a pass-the-parcel, and they need to be protected from germs (although I'm assuming Noa, licked by the dogs from a young age, now has the strongest immune system on the planet). There's no rush, but giving yourself a bit of space and time to just take a few gentle walks (if you're up to it) and learn what you and your baby need is a really good start for your family.

After Noa was born, Emiliana paid us a few visits, bringing groceries to make us fresh juices and helping with vacuuming and arranging into vases all the flowers we'd been sent. Within a week, we'd received so many presents for Noa from family and friends and, on top of that, there was baby paraphernalia everywhere, so the house always looked like a jumble sale and I couldn't help but want to clean. I probably should have stayed in bed a little bit more, but I'm a doer – getting out of bed and coming downstairs to get things done felt like what I should be doing, because that's my personality. I wanted stuff to do. But really I should have been resting, even if I wasn't having a full sleep when Noa slept. I think just lying down or sitting somewhere with your feet up, reading or watching something, looking at your phone while your baby sleeps, just having that down time to rest even if you aren't completely asleep; that will make you feel much better as the days go by than if you do what I did, trying to clean and tidy every time I didn't have Noa on me. The mess can wait, honestly. It isn't going anywhere. When I go to see friends now who have just had babies, my priority is helping with any housework they need doing. Of course I'll be looking forward to seeing their newborn too, but having experienced those first few weeks at home as a new parent, I now understand the importance of the phrase 'it takes a village to raise a child'. (That said, I couldn't believe recently how immaculate my friend's house was when her son was only three weeks old!)

After a couple of days at home, I noticed Noa's finger was really red. The day after that, it was red *and* hot. I called my friend, a nurse, and she said, 'It could be a sign of infection. Call 111.' They sent us straight to A&E, who said it looked like paronychia, common enough in kids when their cuticles or nail beds get infected, but rare in newborns. Because it was an infection, they had to keep her in overnight, so Boj was sent home and I stayed with her while they pumped her with antibiotics.

After two nights we were allowed home, and I tried to relax, even though the antibiotics we were still giving. Noa gave her terrible reflux, and she was projectile vomiting after every feed. After a few nights, she got a temperature. I'd peeked into her Moses basket, and noticed she looked a bit hot.

'Boj? She's sweating. Babies don't sweat.'

Back we went, 11 o'clock at night, and as soon as they heard her history – NICU and the Neo Natal Unit, paronychia and antibiotics – they rushed us straight through. This time, they did lots of tests on her and were ruling things out all the time. Eventually, they pulled me and Boj aside.

'There's a chance it could be sepsis or meningitis. We have to take this really seriously and do more tests, and one of those is a lumbar puncture, a needle through Noa's spine – I'm afraid you're going to have to go because you can't be there for that; the process is quite painful for the baby.' They spoke to us gently. 'Go for a walk outside, get some fresh air if you can.'

So we did. We were both in tears, walking around the grounds of the Whittington, and I vividly remember Boj saying, 'Is she even destined to be here? Is this it?' She'd had problems when she was born, she'd had the infection, and now we were walking around the hospital crying our eyes out and pleading that it wouldn't be sepsis or meningitis.

She was in hospital for two nights, then I had to take her to hospital every day for the following three days and the whole time we were on tenterhooks for the results to come back, while she was being treated as if she did have either sepsis or meningitis, being given hugely strong antibiotics through an IV drip. I just couldn't believe it. I was so grateful for the care she'd received since her very first moments, but I couldn't help thinking too that this was supposed to be the time of our newborn bubble, when our new family was meant to be so happy together. Instead, it had been weeks, and we'd been in and out of hospital and still didn't know if she'd be OK.

Although it's wonderful to see, I still get a gutpunch feeling whenever I see new mums on Instagram having a perfect and happy time during the first couple of weeks after birth, straight home on the day or day after with their healthy, happy baby. Mums with perfect hair, make-up and cheerful captions about being in a newborn bubble of bliss, saying that everything is great, and they've never felt better or more fulfilled. I guess I'm just envious that I never experienced the 'newborn bubble' everyone always seems to talk about. Instead I'd spent the first five days in hospital, my baby was in intensive care, my C-section recovery was painful, and this was followed by two more visits to hospital with potential life-threatening problems for Noa.

Of course, I look back now with a really different perspective. Noa was ill, and the danger to her seemed enormous and terrifying, but there are friends around us who have had a far harder time with their babies, babies who are born with stopped hearts or no oxygen to the brain, friends who have had healthy pregnancies and find in an instant that they are now lifelong carers in a way they had never imagined. But at the time, I had tunnel vision.

When they finally let us leave, still not knowing what it was that Noa had but that it was more likely to be viral and any infection was highly unlikely, we realised that her gut had been really damaged by all the super-strong antibiotics she'd been given since she was born. She couldn't keep anything down, and she looked *tiny*. So we started bottle-feeding her, alongside breastfeeding, trying to get her weight up as much as we could.

Eventually, someone recommended cranial osteopathy. We did three sessions where a woman gently touched Noa's head, and after this she was fully recovered. Of course, it might have sorted itself out anyway on its own in that time – but I didn't want to just do nothing. After all those days of feeling so helpless, I knew we'd try anything to make our daughter feel better.

But what I still can't understand is that as soon as we really got settled at home, and Noa wasn't in hospital any more, and we didn't have to worry about her health being a problem – as soon as that happened, that's when I could feel myself spiralling into a really dark, depressive episode.

A word with . . . Sylvie (my mum)

Even when Kate was little, she wasn't interested in babies. When she and her twin sister were very young, they'd be given dolls, but Kate was always more of a tomboy, more into sport. She loved her brother when he was born, but she was only five and not that bothered by him – she'd rather be playing football or disco dancing. Her sisters loved babies as they got older, but the more time went on, the more clear she was on not ever thinking she'd have them. I got used to that, and was glad for her that she'd made her decision; occasionally I'd ask how she'd feel when she was older and had no family to care for her, but she always had an answer, had definitely thought about it all. I'd also said to her that, if Boj really wanted kids, maybe it wasn't fair to stay with him, but if he really loved her, even not having children, that was a good relationship.

So when she told us she was pregnant, it was a very big shock. I just didn't believe it! Even with the photo from the scan, I didn't believe it, I was just gobsmacked. I was over the moon. I was

convinced she was having a boy, too, because
that's all I could see her with, because she loves
her sport – when she did the gender reveal and
said there was another little girl coming, it was so
lovely.

Her pregnancy was awful for us, not being able
to see her at all because of the pandemic. It was
heartbreaking, because this was her first and she
was older, and a bit scared, so I felt scared too. It
was so different with her sisters because they were
just around the corner for their pregnancies, but
she's over an hour away and that's when we aren't
locked down. I tried to think of ways to help her,
and tried to be on the end of the phone whenever
she needed. She carried brilliantly, though, looked
beautiful and sailed through the whole thing.

But when the baby was born and taken into
NICU, I was so frightened, and with all the
things Noa kept being brought back in with.
Kate was a new mum, and things have changed
so much since I had her and her sisters and
brother, and I felt awful I couldn't be with her,
couldn't go to the hospital or help her out when
she came home. It was hard.

Some of the things she'd put on Instagram made me really worried. I'd ask her how she was, but I could see something wasn't right, and there was so little I could do. I could only advise her on what had worked for me, when I'd had my C-sections, but she was back and forth to the hospital on her own, and some of the tests on Noa were so serious. I got so scared for Kate at one stage because I could see how low she was, but still didn't realise how bad it was until later. Everyone keeps things from their mums to stop them worrying, but I did get upset at how low she'd been. All I could do at the time was say to her, 'I'm here for you, whatever you want, whatever we can do, we'll do.' It felt like everything was against us, trying to help Kate and Boj and Noa.

In normal times, I'd have been round there, putting her to bed, looking after Noa, dealing with it all to help her. But she was getting advice from all these different places, because parenting advice changes over time, doesn't it, and my views weren't always the same as theirs. I could see how much struggle she was having with breastfeeding, and I wanted to reassure her that going onto the bottle had never done her or her siblings any harm.

I look at her now and I think she's the most fantastic mum. I'm so shocked, but I knew she'd fall in love. When you get your own child, it's completely different! I can see how much more she enjoys it now, compared to at the beginning when it was all worrying and learning. She's so hands-on with Noa, and the three of them are so happy. It's brilliant.

7

Dark Times

.

The first few weeks were surprisingly tough. I kept waiting for us to get into a rhythm with Noa, but nothing was clicking. What had seemed so easy to begin with was only getting harder – she had reflux, constipation, trapped wind, latching issues, and she was barely sleeping, which meant neither was I.

There were times – like everyone had, of course, in 2020 – when I felt so isolated. Friends would ring the doorbell with gifts or delicious homemade food and we'd have a doorstep chat down the path and they'd wave at Noa, but no one could cuddle her or get close. That's the only experience I'll ever have with a newborn. And it did make my mental health at the time a bit worse each day, as I just wanted to hug my friends and invite them in for a chat and a cuppa.

One day our doorbell rang and when Boj opened the

front door, nobody was there, but on our doorstep was a bag with a card and a really warm tin inside. (Don't panic, it wasn't dog shit.) Boj opened the tin and there was an absolutely stunning-smelling loaf of blueberry, almond, and lemon cake, and the card said, 'To Kate and Boj, congratulations on the birth of Noa! It's great to have neighbours like you. Just give us a holler if ever you need us, hope you enjoy the cake. Rachel, Dave and the kids.'

I didn't know a Rachel on this street. We'd not met a Dave either. We'd also not waved or said hi to any couple with their kids. My paranoia was getting the better of me.

'These sound like made-up names. I think someone's followed us, found out where we live and they're trying to poison us. We CANNOT eat that cake!'

Boj looked at the cake again. 'Are you *sure* you don't know a Rachel?'

Then I suddenly realised: it was a friend of a friend called Rachel, who I'd only been introduced to on WhatsApp (and never knew her husband was called Dave). I couldn't stop laughing and felt such a knob for having such irrational thoughts about a stranger attempting to kill us with cake. As soon as I placed her and realised someone wasn't trying to actively murder us,

I *ran* to that cake and scoffed the biggest slice with my hands like a wild pig. But a moment before, I was shaking with fear that someone was trying to kill me and my family. Funny what sleep deprivation does to you.

In fact, I was becoming more and more miserable. I was crying every day, for most of the day, and through the night, when I'd be awake and trying to feed Noa for hours at a time. I didn't want to get out of bed. I felt like I was completely losing my mind.

I googled suicide. I googled suicide rates among new mums and was shocked to find out that in the UK and Ireland, maternal suicide is the leading cause of direct deaths occurring within a year after the end of pregnancy. In fact, in a 2018 report by MBRRACE-UK,[1] they found that around 20 out of 120 deaths of women who took their own lives did so between the periods of six weeks and one year after pregnancy. I felt devastated for their families and deeply sad that I could relate to how they felt. There were times during the first twelve weeks of Noa's life that I genuinely didn't want to be here any more. I used to stare at her breastfeeding and I'd be in floods of tears stroking her head because I couldn't understand how I could love something so much, with

1 Mothers and Babies: Reducing Risk through Audits and Confidential Enquiries Across the UK

every fibre of my being, yet feel so unhappy at the same time. I felt that I'd not only ruined my life, I'd ruined Noa's, I'd ruined Boj's, I ruined our relationship, and the dog's lives. From the good start I'd made with Noa feeding, breastfeeding was becoming more and more of an issue. I desperately wanted to keep doing it – with Boj's mum saying, 'Breast is best, you must breastfeed! It's the best protection for the baby!' – and my own mum saying, 'Just get a bottle, put her on formula.' Like millions of mums before me, I felt a failure, that I'd let Noa down, as my milk supply dwindled from a waterboarding gush at the start that would often leave Noa choking, and freezing bags and bags of it, to really struggling to feel like Noa was getting enough at each feed. I still enjoyed the closeness of it, but now Noa would sometimes get on my boob and after only a moment start fussing and crying. Almost everyone was telling me to stop, to take the pressure off myself, but I couldn't see things that way: all I could see was that I was letting Noa down, and that I alone had made this choice which was ruining the lives of everyone I loved.

I was staying in my pyjamas all day, every day. I wasn't showering. I managed to brush my teeth, but sometimes it wouldn't be until past lunchtime, and only to make up for the enormous amount of food I was eating, which Boj was cooking for me, three times a day, to try and lift my strength and my spirits. Everything with Noa was so new, and so terrifying. How do I wind her? How do I stop her crying? What should I use to help her reflux and constipation? When should I swaddle her? Nothing was coming to me naturally. Even though I still felt that bond with her, and was still totally obsessed with her, I had no confidence about anything I was doing or any choice I was making. I never knew what to dress her in, which sounds silly; but I would see immaculately dressed newborn babies on Instagram and all I had the energy to do was put her in a babygro, which then made me feel lazy. Then I was frustrated as I was never sure if she was wearing enough layers or too many layers. Looking back, these were such minor issues, but they felt like such a big deal and kept taking me back to that negative thought process – that I was a bad mum with no idea what I was doing – and I felt paralysed by constantly second-guessing myself. And without the confidence that we were doing OK, Boj and I would start digging at each other – have you sterilised this? No, I don't know how to sterilise. Can you do that? Well, how do you do it? I don't know, how should I know?

We were hugely sleep-deprived, we were frightened and frustrated, and I realise now that we had also been traumatised by Noa's illnesses in the first weeks of her life. But instead of recognising the fact that we had our heads screwed on our shoulders and plenty of people we knew had learned all this parenting stuff too, all I could see was that I couldn't meet Noa's needs, and I couldn't see that changing any time soon. I was making life harder for myself too, in countless tiny ways: Noa had a dummy to sleep at that stage, but I hadn't clicked that she only wanted it to sleep, so would spend my day tearfully and frustratedly putting it back in her mouth every time she spat it out. Why? Why did I do that? That's what happens when you're too sleep-deprived to think properly.

The visits from the health visitor didn't help. I know some women have had amazing experiences with their health visitor when their baby was born, but I've got to be honest, looking back, I'm quite shocked that she didn't, or wouldn't, recognise how badly I was struggling, and how blasé she was about how I looked. Each time she visited, my eyes would be red from crying, my hair greasy, my skin pale, with one boob out, trying to feed and failing, clearly getting no rest at all. All she would say each time was, 'You're doing really good, keep going, all this is totally normal! It's just the baby blues!'

Which of course made me feel worse. She may have been trying to reassure me, but all I could think was that the baby blues is nothing, everyone gets over the baby blues, it doesn't sit with them for weeks and weeks and weeks like this, they get over it and move on, so I was failing at that too. And if this was 'normal', did that mean I was going to feel like this for the rest of my life? Crying, failing, regretful, hating myself, feeling so guilty at what I was doing to Noa and Boj, never able to be any kind of mother to Noa? This was *normal*?

I wasn't even sleeping when Noa slept, which might have helped me, but when you're that tired you no longer make sensible choices. Instead, Noa would be put down for a nap and I'd rush around the house, trying to make a dent in the terrible mess it had become since we'd come back from the hospital, trying to do one of the few things I'd previously been able to do perfectly well – but I was so tired, I couldn't even do that. And still, the health visitor never sat with me, never asked, 'Really, how do you feel right now? Do you ever feel like you don't want to be here any more? How much of the day do you spend feeling like this? Would you like me to refer you to your GP for some help?' I realise this isn't the primary job of a health visitor and perhaps she didn't see the signs, but I found it so difficult to say out loud how I was feeling. I just wanted her to ask me, because for some stupid reason, if she'd have asked me I'd probably have told her. I know that sounds ridiculous, but it's true. Me, loud mouth Mary, Mouth of the South, confident Kate, not even able to say those words; but it's an issue I've always struggled with as an adult – making the first move to tell someone how I'm really feeling. I know so many people are nervous of talking about suicide because they're terrified that even saying the word will make it happen somehow, that using the word suicide to somebody will make that person instantly suicidal. But that's part of the stigma of suicide that so many campaigners are trying to break, and I know it would have made an enormous difference to me if that was part of the questions I'd been asked as a new mum, by someone who was willing to not just listen, but actually pay attention to how I was feeling. As it was, the health visitor each time just said, 'Keep doing what you're doing . . .' And I would let her out and have another cry.

I didn't get diagnosed for a long time. It was that stigma again – I have always seen myself as strong-minded, positive and outgoing, the silly and happy one, which obviously is total bullshit when it comes to any kind of depression. Depression at any time, in any situation, is an illness, and like any illness, anyone can get it, and because I'd never even entertained the idea when I was pregnant I might get post-natal depression – it must have been one of the few things I hadn't worried about – I didn't go to the doctor to get the treatment I needed.

I was so convinced everyone felt like this and just got over it, because no one had ever said to me that they felt this bad. It must be normal: I'd had a baby in the height of a global pandemic, she'd had repeated hospital stays with breathing issues and infection and suspected sepsis/meningitis, and my family couldn't visit so I couldn't get that extra support. The truth probably is that I just didn't want to believe that I needed help. I thought I was being strong, refusing to realise I needed someone to help me, but actually it was the PND talking, because depression lies about everything: who you are, what you need, and what everyone else feels about you too.

I went to bed every night thinking, *Tomorrow has to be better. I'm sure I'll feel better then.* But when I woke up there were still feeding issues (which family members continued to weigh in on, and I know they thought they were trying to help but still . . .) and the constant tiredness, and the crying, the reflux, the vomiting, tears and screaming. No day ever felt better than the day before.

When I woke up each morning, straight away there was a sadness and an anxiety. I'd think, *Is today going to be any better? Am I going to get through it without crying?* Everything was just soaked in this feeling of regret and that I'd made a huge mistake, and if I wasn't happy how badly would that be damaging Noa? So I'd be trying to put on a brave face, terrified I was really causing Noa future damage, but every day I felt the same and every day Noa was suffering with reflux and pain, and a tongue tie that wasn't diagnosed for some months.

I just remember this constant sadness, a sense that now I was going to be miserable forever. I couldn't see a way. I couldn't see me ever enjoying motherhood, even with all the messages saying, 'I promise you, it gets easier and I promise you it gets better, and I promise you, you won't feel like this forever.' But I didn't know if I'd be here in a week's time, let alone in six months. I was drowning, all the time.

Only when I went to the GP for Noa's six-week jabs did anyone besides Boj and my family begin to notice something was wrong. And even then, I was too proud to ask for help. There's also something in our British stiff-upper-lip thing where people are often scared to ask if you need help – that if they ask you whether you're feeling really bad, or even suicidal, it might offend you somehow or will make you feel much worse than you already do, so it's better to just say, 'Don't worry, you'll be OK in a bit.' Really, it's always better to ask, from either side. The nurse asked me how I was, and I said, 'Fine,' then immediately burst into tears. All I could say was, 'It's just so *hard*,' and she took it more seriously, but still said how normal it was to feel that way, with sleep deprivation, and the pandemic, and lockdown rules. I remember her saying, 'If you keep feeling like this, if you feel like this every day without a change, then please come back again, we will try to help,' but I stupidly didn't go back.

And my guilt wasn't just about Noa, but about the position that I was complaining from: Boj was running his own business, so he was able to take longer paternity leave be at home to help. I wasn't physically damaged by the birth. Noa seemed unlikely to return to hospital. How could I talk about how hard all this was when I had a secure roof over our heads, good health for me and Boj and Noa, loving family and friends, even if we couldn't see them, food on the table, bills paid, jobs we liked, running water, peaceful streets, all of the privilege we enjoyed – how could I dare say it was hard when there would be, at that very moment, thousands of women struggling in practical ways I couldn't even imagine? So I didn't chase it up. I just kept waiting, because people kept saying, 'Oh, the first month is hard. The first six weeks are difficult. Just get through the first three months, the first four months are the ones that will really get you.' So I kept waiting and waiting and waiting, for this corner to turn and to feel differently, to feel I was doing OK and it was worth me being here for Noa, that I wasn't making things worse for her by being in her life.

The point of depression is that it's an illness that can happen to anyone. Look at any list of celebrities who have suffered from PND: Adele, Stacey Solomon, Cardi B, Gwyneth Paltrow, Serena Williams – money and position might protect you from practical worries around homelessness and paying the bills, but it doesn't make the depression and related conditions any less crippling. It might be easier to access support and care at that level, but no one with depression wakes up on the first morning with it and says, 'I know what this is! I'll get some therapy and medication this afternoon!' And when you're also supposed to be caring for a baby, it's even more pressure and stress, whatever the size of your house and the number of followers you have on Instagram. But the more we talk about it, the signs and symptoms, the things you *don't* have to go through as 'normal', the more we might help women to ask for help sooner, or have those people around her recognise it and get help on her behalf.

It's hard to talk about that level of exhaustion to people who aren't experiencing it right now. Even if you've had it in the past, I think you forget – your brain can't hold on to memories of that kind of tiredness. And I'd be getting no sleep, then performing so hard for Noa every day, singing and playing and trying to go full-blast as a fun mum-slash-children's entertainer (I've recently been told there's no point me having Botox again, since I'm working my face so hard with Noa that it just wears off too fast, which I couldn't help but find hilarious), it was just mentally and physically exhausting.

Someone told me in my last month of pregnancy that I'd sleep so much better once Noa was born. The bump wouldn't be in the way, the baby wouldn't be kicking me, I shouldn't let anyone scare me about never sleeping again. How I wish that were true. I'd got my hopes up and foolishly believed I'd feel more rested once Noa was born, and while some newborns are great sleepers, our baby wasn't. Consequently, I was enormously sleep-deprived. If parenting was a paid job, there's no way your boss would allow you to work if you'd repeatedly had only a couple of hours sleep. They'd say, 'You need to take a break, you need a rest, you need a day off, it's not safe for you to be working in this condition.' But instead, we're beyond tired, getting only broken sleep night after night, and then we're handed these tiny vulnerable babies to take care of. 'Oh, you'll be fine, you had two hours' sleep yesterday, crack on.' Sleep deprivation is a form of torture, and I felt like I was being tortured. I couldn't even begin to think straight.

It would make me cry every time I looked at Noa, because I loved her so much but I couldn't make her stop crying, and I'd be thinking, *You're so upset, and* nothing *I'm doing is making you feel any better*. I knew it wasn't her fault, but I couldn't see it wasn't my fault either – and resentment grew, resentment towards Boj. He was the one who had wanted this baby for years, who'd convinced me that I'd be a great mum and it would be the best thing for us both, but he was the one sleeping and I wasn't. So I tried to do it all alone, feeling guilty that I felt this way, that I had regrets about this baby who I loved more than anything in the world, but still I was getting lower and lower and didn't want to be there any more.

Then of course as soon as I thought about me not being there, I'd look at her, my whole world in this beautiful little potato, and think about who would look after her if I wasn't there, and I'd cry more. She was so helpless and had no way of communicating with us apart from crying her eyes out, and I couldn't make her feel any better and so felt worse and worse myself. How awful was I to regret having her? Sometimes that crying still happens: now when I'm due on and it's been a tough day, on my own, I still cry a little bit, but it's nothing like that dark time. Part of the difficulty now is that I make it harder for myself, always going at a hundred miles an hour, singing songs and doing dances, but at least she can communicate so much more and she's no longer a newborn.

I'd look at her and feeling that overwhelming love, but also regret and anxiety, and stress and sadness, worrying about what damage it was doing to Noa to see me crying every day, because of course it would have an effect on her. So I'd be sitting with her, silently bawling while trying to breastfeed, and she'd be refusing my boobs and crying. There would be milk coming out of my boobs and she'd still be refusing them, only wanting a bottle, and I'd be so angry. This is the one reason we've got boobs! I felt so rejected. Why don't you want my milk? Is there not enough? Are you uncomfortable in this position? Do my nipples smell? *What am I doing wrong?*

After the first short while of successful feeding and flow, where I had so much milk, it then dwindled under stress and I was having all-day pumping sessions, trying to build the supply back up, unable to do anything else but pump all day, just chained to the house because I was either feeding – or trying to feed – or expressing. One minute she'd be feeding, the next she'd be screaming and wanting a bottle.

I found myself thinking, day after day, *Why have we done this?* Even though my pregnancy and Noa's birth had been such a joy, I was aware that Boj was feeling bad, for asking me to do this for so many years, when I kept saying I didn't want to, and then he was trying to go back to work and do his job *and* support me, and I was just falling apart and blaming him. He could disappear off to the office and have interactions with other adults, and I was at home all day with a baby that I was desperate to have in some kind of feeding and napping routine when in fact she was far too young to be in one. I was so anxious about driving anywhere with her in case she cried in the car seat or had a meltdown in front of my family or friends, I had so many insecurities and emotions going round and round in my head, and I felt so incompetent. People said I just needed to get through those months, but I had day after day of thinking, *How am I supposed to get through the next twenty-four hours*, and there were moments I felt like I genuinely didn't want to be alive any more. That the only way I could possibly stop feeling like this was to kill myself.

The stress of feeling like I was going to lose Boj was also massive. A friend said this to me just before Noa was born: 'When you've got a newborn, you've got to reset at the end of every day and forget any arguments or harsh words that were exchanged because you'll both say things you don't really mean. Try not to nitpick about who has done more nappy changes, or washing up, or who has had less sleep and when the baby's crying you're both going to be stressed, so just try to have patience with each other.' And Boj has patience in spades, so yet again it was me letting the side down. I wasn't resetting every day. One night after what felt like hours of trying to stop Noa crying on my own in her nursery while Boj was fast asleep, I remember rushing into the bedroom and literally screaming 'I can't do this any more!' and I put Noa down on the bed firmly in a way that made me realise I was so close to shaking her, and I ran upstairs to our loft, so scared at what I'd nearly done. Boj came and found me, on my knees, sobbing, saying over and over again, 'I can't do it, I can't do it any more, I can't do it any more . . .'

He took over, he put Noa to bed, he took me down to the kitchen, made me toasted hot cross buns, then we got back into bed and watched back-to-back episodes of a new sitcom we'd recently discovered, with me laughing and crying simultaneously, until I kept saying to him, 'What did you just say?' when he hadn't said anything, or replying to things that he hadn't said. Boj said, 'I think you're so sleep-deprived you're delusional. Let's get you to bed. I'll give her a bottle – this isn't healthy, Kate. You can't do this on your own.' He was so patient with both of us, maybe because he didn't see us twenty-four hours a day, but his levels of tolerance were so different to mine. And I was so grateful. I mean, I've always been thankful to be with someone so calm, but even more so seeing him with Noa, how gentle and patient he was, even when she'd cry for hours for no reason we could work out. The more I watched him, the more I knew he was absolutely the only person I could ever have had a baby with.

A word with . . . Kate S (my best friend)

I've known Katie for at least fifteen years now, and she's basically got two extremes: so hilarious and always going at a hundred miles an hour, and being one of the most caring people I know. She's really sensitive and has this amazing soft side that you see when she's with the dogs, for instance. She goes out of her way for friends and family, she's so thoughtful and always has time for you (even if she can be pretty shit at answering the phone, because she's always keeping herself so busy).

I think she'd convinced herself that she never wanted a kid because she didn't want one in her twenties, back when we first met, but her maternal side was clear to see when she was with Baxter and Shirley. When we lived near each other in London (from 2015, two years before my daughter was born, until I moved away in 2019), we saw each other every day, meeting up for morning, child-free dog walks. We continued to do this while I was pregnant, so Kate really got the low-down on what it was like, and then our walking crew was extended by one as I had my daughter in the pushchair. I think this was the first time Kate was ever close enough to actually see a baby regularly. To see the way Kate was with her – it made my heart melt. Kate always makes out she's so blasé, but when she had to babysit for the first time ever, she was terrified about doing it right. I could see that caring side in her, and I remember Boj saying to me that he thought my baby might have been a turning point for Kate. Then when my daughter got a little bit older, Kate and Boj took her for fish and chips and to the park and began to see you could still have fun, and even still go down the pub, with your baby. And they loved it. Yes, having a baby affects your life, but that's a good thing. Isn't it?

Kate had the normal worries that every mum has through pregnancy, but she looked great, felt great. At one point she talked about the insomnia, and I just thought, *You don't know yet, Kate.* Before Noa was born, I said to them, 'You just do what it takes to survive,' and Boj said, 'That's a bit extreme! There's two of us and only one of them, I think we'll be fine.'

Once Noa was born, Katie was so anxious. She's always had that anxious predisposition, but it hadn't impacted her life that much; after Noa was born she would FaceTime me every single day, partly because I'm a paediatric nurse, and partly because my younger daughter is exactly a year older than Noa, so I'd been through it all relatively recently. She'd come to me for all this advice, and I'd keep thinking that *we* didn't know what we were doing either, but I answered every call and tried to tell her how it all was. There are some mums who are full Gina Ford and do all the controlled crying, and others who breastfed until the kids are five – there's no right or wrong way, is there, it's just what you want to do.

But because she'd never really been around babies, Kate was asking questions about absolutely everything, like how to feed the baby, how to burp the baby, because she'd never taken any of that on when she was around other babies. Everything was a major decision to make, and she's so reactive that if something didn't work one day, she'd be off trying to find another solution because that one had failed, and Noa was still crying or waking up in the night. Even when Noa was a healthy baby, growing really well, Kate thought things were still going wrong. She said she just had no fucking idea, but that's normal, because generally you *don't* have any idea. Kate's personality means that she always wanted an answer to everything, to change things to get the right outcome, and sometimes there just wasn't one. You just have to go with it, don't you?

You don't want to give your own opinions to your friends, not least because they might not want what you want from parenting, but she was listening to everything I said, so I had to be so careful. She just needed reassurance, like any new mum, but then on top of that she was saying she really wasn't enjoying any of it. And I was the same – I struggled so much for the first six months of both babies, because they're so little at that age and they don't give anything back, so I knew exactly how she was feeling. Plus, I think I felt responsible; I'd said, 'You're going to love having kids, it's great!' And now she was really struggling, and I didn't want to make her feel worse.

People talk about that magical time with a newborn, and I was like, 'What magical time? My fanny's falling out. I've got something sucking on my tits. I'm arguing with my boyfriend, I don't know what day it is, and I've not brushed my teeth in a week. Magical time . . .'

At one point I told her to go to the GP and tell them that she might need some help, but Kate's not like that; she'd try every single last other thing before she'd admit how she was feeling. I tried to tell her that she wasn't failing, but it was all just such a struggle for her, particularly in the pandemic without her normal network of friends around. Siobhan was really good support for her, because she was so experienced and completely present.

I look at Kate now, and she's so far out of the fog. She's getting sleep, she's back at work, she's enjoying Noa so much more, and she's done such a good job. I don't think she could see how well she was doing, and that was always heartbreaking. It's so nice that she's back to being able to care about other people again, and she's able to offer what she's learned to other friends who are going through it. For the next few years, my advice to her would be: just try to breathe. Do what you want to do for your family, and be aware that once they're fully mobile it's a lot more demanding. They're a lot more fun as they get older, but there'll still be teething issues and other things, and if they have one good night's sleep then be glad of that one night. And always, always carry loads of snacks.

8

Taking Steps

My family are a really close family, living around the corner from each other, so even in lockdown we'd be talking every day on our group WhatsApp, 'Keeping Up With The Lawlers'. I was able to see my twin sister, Karen, most Fridays as she began cleaning for us once a week when Noa was born, which was amazing. Even though we had things like FaceTime, I missed seeing my family in person so much – occasionally they'd see something on my Instagram, and get in touch to say, 'Are you OK?' but just as I didn't put everything on Insta, I didn't tell them everything either. The first time they were able to come and meet Noa, it was also the first time I'd seen them in such a long time. My parents walked in and I gave my dad the biggest hug. I just fell into his arms and couldn't stop crying. I was so overwhelmed to see them both, and I think they'd known I was struggling but it was only at that moment when they realised how serious it was. I didn't realise until I was physically hugging them both just how much I needed to be in their arms. I could tell they were quite shocked; I think they're so used to me being loud and outgoing and silly, but now I was sobbing like mad. Me, Mum and Dad stood there hugging together for the longest time, and I could feel my dad trying his hardest to hold it together but I could sense that it really upset him seeing his daughter so emotionally broken. I'll never forget that moment, how grateful I felt to have such loving parents who were there for me when I needed them the most. I remember thinking in that moment, *I've got to keep living. I can't leave Noa, Boj, Baxter and Shirley, and I can't ever do that to my parents.* Sometimes even when you're a grown-up, nothing beats a cuddle from your mum and dad. We took so many photos that day, and it reminded me that even if we have arguments, like all families – Brexit was an interesting time – we do love each other so much.

In April, we met up outdoors, and I curled my hair and had a spray tan. Noa had fed really well that day and it was one of the first times I'd made a real effort since she was born, and for those few hours I began to see a tiny sliver of hope. Mostly I lived in pyjamas in those first few months, no make-up, looking like I'd been dug up. It just felt too much effort to shower some days, and what was I supposed to do with Noa when I was showering? It seemed impossible. I know this might sound ridiculous but the idea of just putting her in her baby chair felt too much of a worry at the time, I thought she'd cry, so any rare chance I had to see my family was a way to kick myself into washing and dressing.

But they still all lived well over an hour away, and we were still under lockdown, pretty much, so that one day wasn't enough to keep me going longer term. My brother and big sister didn't meet Noa for over a month, when she'd already grown so much, and that was hard. None of them knew I was having suicidal feelings through those months; my twin sister probably saw me at my lowest, because she was coming every week and I was always in tears, unwashed. But still I never gave her the chance to know how bad I was feeling. I was so low; I couldn't tell them how bad it was. It's one thing to say, 'Oh, I've had a shit day at work, and I missed the train and I burnt the tea,' but it's so much harder to get into a conversation about how you can't stop thinking about ending your own life. Trying to get perspective, but never finding it.

Every week I'd get these emails from the NHS about progress and check-ups for Noa, and at the foot of every single one there was a reminder to never shake your baby, no matter what happens. NSPCC research suggests that there have been over 220 deaths from shaken baby syndrome in the UK over the last ten years, and in those moments with Noa where I'd been so desperate, so out of my mind, I can see why it's so, so, so important that people have ways of asking for help. It's essential people have a way of stepping away, even for five minutes, to reset themselves, but even better to get proper support so they are never pushed to the edge in that way.

In the end, I did three things that seemed to start turning things around: I accepted Boj's suggestion of having a night nanny three nights a week until I felt better; I began to see a therapist; and I continued to talk honestly about how I was feeling on Instagram.

First, we found Siobhan, a night nanny in our area, and she changed our lives monumentally. When Noa was five weeks old, Siobhan would arrive in the evening three times each week, and we were supposed to go straight to bed while she took care of Noa and we slept, but she was so knowledgeable and supportive that we'd often stay up late, chatting to her and asking her all sorts of questions about caring for Noa: 'She's started doing this – what does that mean?' It was Siobhan that spotted Noa's posterior tongue-tie, something that my GP told me wasn't there, enabling us to get it snipped at six weeks and improve Noa's feeding. She gave us suggestions about how to put Noa down into her Moses basket asleep in order for her to not wake up, what to swaddle her in, how to notice when she was tired, how to cope with her crying; there were breastfeeding tips, nappy-changing tips, tips on how to communicate with Noa, what sensory toys to show her, what sounds to play her – she gave us so many tools that meant I could start feeling like I had a handle on being a mother; I started to believe that maybe I could care for Noa in the way I knew she deserved. When we see Siobhan now, she says she still meets clients who have seen her on my Instagram and got in touch to ask for her help. I know that we wouldn't have got through those four months without her. Suddenly we had a baby and parenting expert in our house three times a week, it was like a fountain of knowledge with total calmness as well. You can go to all the antenatal classes (of which we did none, because of COVID-19), read all the books (I read one and a half) and watch all the YouTube videos (probably watched a few more of these), but until you've got a baby, you just don't know how it's going to be.

I've said to my best friend that I want to give her a session with a doula or lactation consultant when her baby is born, because it was so helpful, and I want to do more than give her a babygro that will only be used for a few weeks. I've suggested that she get home and give everything a try first, because it's almost more helpful for them to come after a few weeks when you've worked out any issues or questions you might have. 'Am I doing this right? Can you show me a different hold position?' I learned so much from Siobhan, and we'd get a decent night's sleep, just waking up once to express milk for the next day. It's not affordable for everyone, I know, but in terms of how much it helped us as a family, it was the best investment that would directly benefit Noa. Despite my stubbornness of wanting to try and do it alone, I'm so glad that Boj pushed me to consider it, because it's so easy to disappear down an internet rabbit hole that will just make you panic and spiral even further out of control. It's such a modern idea that we're just meant to parent alone – there's a reason we've raised kids in close communities forever, with parents and cousins and neighbours all around you, all helping and supporting you. I truly believe it takes a village.

It *does* get easier, and it does get better, but the point is you don't know that at the time, and it seems like an impossibly long way away if you don't have help and support. One moment I remember where I was able to laugh like the old days through my overwhelmingly dark mood was when the *Daily Mail* decided to do an article on our night nanny – and the comments on there! My god! 'No wonder her baby doesn't want her boobs any more, because she's not even f***ing feeding it!' I didn't want to lie about getting help, though; we have friends who have nannies five days a week but keep it on the down low, but I never wanted to give the impression on social media that I was coping better with Noa by doing it on my own. I know the people commenting on those articles wouldn't bat an eyelid if my mum or sister were staying with us overnight to help. We were in the middle of a pandemic, my parents were forbidden from visiting as they weren't in our bubble, and this was the only way we could get the support we needed. It was expensive – even those three nights a week we had Siobhan took all of my statutory maternity pay – but it was important to me to say to people at the time: right now I need help, and help is the only thing making a difference to us as a family.

I only know now that you can ask your midwife for a lactation consultant. Once you've had the baby, you can book in a half hour appointment with someone who'll come to your house and check positioning, latching, how you're holding the baby, how the baby's mouth is working. Everyone tells you how difficult it is to breast-feed, but nobody told me how difficult it is to stop. I never expected for me or Noa to seemingly get the hang of it as quickly as we did, or for my supply to be as good as it was in those first few weeks; I couldn't believe how overwhelmingly connected I felt to her whenever she fed from me and I really surprised myself with how happy the whole process made me feel. I thought Noa's feeding was going great, until it wasn't. I cherished it so much in the beginning, and I wasn't prepared for how rejected, upset and frustrated I would feel when she decided she didn't want me in that way any more.

There's so much pressure for women to breastfeed – to give their babies the 'liquid gold', particularly at the very start – but the support of a qualified lactation consultant makes such a difference. The bonding is magical too, feeding a baby from your body, but even when we switched to bottles, I'd feed Noa with my top off for that skin-to-skin contact. Don't let anyone make you feel you should or shouldn't be doing it, as long as you and the baby are being cared for; the struggle of breastfeeding and having Noa reject my boobs, crying and banging at them, made me so upset with her and with myself, like I was failing her. You might be wondering if I regret persisting with it and driving myself crazy expressing and chaining myself indoors to feed then pump, feed then pump, feed then pump until, before I knew it, we were going to bed again. The answer is no, because I wanted to do everything in my power to continue breastfeeding, to feed and nourish my daughter the way I wanted to – but it wasn't meant to be. When I eventually realised that it wasn't *my* decision to make any more, that it was Noa's and I should do the right thing as her mum and feed her the way *she* wanted to be fed, it was much easier to accept and move on with formula. Only now do I fully understand that a fed baby is a happy baby. Bottle or breast, as long as they're getting their milk, that's great. I was far too stubborn about breastfeeding, when it's such a tiny part of their lives. If it doesn't work for you, it will still be OK.

The second thing actually came from the *Celebrity Bumps* show. We were scheduled to film a post-birth section at home and do a really long interview, and I was late – I'd never been late for filming throughout the entire process – because Noa wouldn't settle and I was trying to feed and the whole afternoon I kept having to having to redo my make-up because I was so upset that Noa was interrupting filming, and I was also getting highly emotional answering questions in the interview. We took some photos that day and I'm amazed that I look like a proper functioning human in them, but from the moment the crew arrived until they left, I was on edge and feeling like I wanted to burst into tears. It was one of my lowest points. The series producer called us up the next day and said, 'Kate, we can see you're having a bit of a tough time at the moment, and we want to offer you some counselling.' I agreed to do it, but I don't think I ever intended to actually see the counsellor; it was Boj who pushed and pushed, and eventually presented me with a therapist he was recommended by the show's psychologist that he thought might work for me. He knew how, despite me being such a chatterbox, I find it so hard to talk properly about my feelings, even in a relationship or with my closest friends, let alone with a total stranger I was paying.

That first meeting with Anna when Noa was seven weeks old was like a weight had been lifted. After only an hour, I felt so much better. We spoke every week and she, like Siobhan, offered me tools to start helping myself. And having a professional listen to everything we'd been through, and diagnose me not only with post-natal depression but also with generalised anxiety disorder, made me cry and cry at that feeling of being heard, not having to filter myself to protect my friends or family, not having to worry about what this person thought of me; she could just listen with experience and advice. It's difficult for me to even write this here – despite everything, I am so private about these bits of my life on social media. I was so uncomfortable covering some of this with Anna as she teased out information from me with questionnaires and got me to scale my feelings from 1 to 10. But I want mums to know that these are issues many of us struggle with, and that you can get help for them, and there is no shame in asking for help. It's what professionals are there for, especially when you're not able to get support from parents or siblings. We were never meant to raise our children in units of two or three people, but now we move around the world so independently and don't have a strong system around us of people who have known us for years, so we don't necessarily want to ask for help. If you can access it, therapy is amazing for anyone – I was so reluctant to pay someone to listen to me moan, but I can't tell you how much it improved things for me. It might be hard, and I know for financial reasons it's not an option for lots of people when the waiting list for therapy via the NHS is sometimes months if not years, but it's really worth it.

Of course, social media has its issues, but the third thing that helped me at this point was the amazing mums of Instagram. In some of my darkest moments, I could open the app at 3 a.m. and talk instantly about issues with feeding or sleeping, and there would be so many women who were also awake, who'd say, 'I've got the same thing! I'm so glad I'm not alone!' and I'd be thinking the same thing: *Thank God I'm not alone.* This 'Wide Awake Club' I'd become part of meant I was able to chat to an incredible bunch of people via Stories, Q&As and DMs, where I'd reply to as many as I could, until it was time to get some more sleep. I was finding what felt like an army of women in the same boat with babies, toddlers and young kids, admitting they too were finding it overwhelmingly difficult being a mum, or feeling as though they were failing. I couldn't ring my mum in the middle of the night, or chat to my mates at silly o'clock, but I had this enormous group of friends I could chat to at any hour, and we'd share this shit that we were wading through together. Those actually became some of my favourite moments, snuggling in a dark nursery with Noa, feeling connected, even through my misery, with this funny, caring, wide-awake club.

I wasn't as honest on there as I was with Anna – I never spoke about feeling suicidal. But I said, 'If you're crying every day, I'm here with you. If you're wondering how you're going to cope through the next week, I'm here too.' I received hundreds of messages, not just from parents going through it at the time, but also from parents saying they'd been in that place a year or two years before, even twenty years before, and wished they'd known someone else at the time who felt how they did, that I somehow made them realise that how they were feeling wasn't so unusual. So I felt like I had a responsibility to keep being honest about my struggles, as honest as I could be in order to help others. Even one of my oldest, bestest friends messaged me saying, 'I felt the same with my first.' But she hadn't said anything at the time. I had no idea she ever struggled when she became a mum for the first time. 'No one else felt that way, so I didn't feel like I could say anything,' she explained. That's the trouble – we see these perfect portrayals of motherhood in the tabloids, magazines and on social media, with perfectly dressed babies and immaculate-looking homes, new mums out and about, attending events or flying abroad so soon after giving birth. Meanwhile, you still haven't left the house or got dressed for the second day running, so it's hard not to feel that you're doing it wrong. I often think of that Robin Williams quote: 'All it takes is a beautiful fake smile to hide an injured soul, and they will never notice how broken you really are.' How many of our pictures on social media are just beautiful fake smiles, hiding how much we're all struggling? Everyone talks about the joy of the newborn bubble – I mean, this book could almost have been called *What Fucking Newborn Bubble?* Because I never got that, and I've been inundated with messages from parents in similar situations who never got their newborn bubble either. It's not a given. There is no automatic newborn bubble, but it does exist for some and if it's blissful from the moment you arrive home with your baby then you're one lucky ducky, my friend.

I know some new mums have amazing pregnancies, great labours, feel incredible afterwards, going on holiday, to awards ceremonies or parties and making huge gorgeous celebratory lunches for friends and families the day after their baby has been born, T H R I V I N G – and good for them. But it still hurts me when I see that. Not that it means they shouldn't talk about it, I just wish I had a different experience and enjoyed the newborn days more. Because for every mum for whom it all went brilliantly and who wants to celebrate it, there are plenty of parents who are also having a miserable time, who are losing their minds, worried about their baby and their relationship, their mental health, their physical health, who might have wanted a baby for a long time or found themselves unexpectedly pregnant, and now have had their lives flipped upside down and don't know how they're ever going to carry on to the next day. I just wanted to be a voice saying, 'If you feel shit, come and sit with me, and we can try and get through it together.' It was nice to have somewhere to laugh at those times when people would say: 'Make the most of these days, you'll miss them when they're gone!' I could not disagree more. Those newborn days were so intense, so incredibly difficult, the hardest thing I've ever done. I lost every bit of myself, and lived in constant fear of what I might do at any moment; my boobs weren't working, the baby was throwing up every five minutes, I could barely shower or brush my teeth, nothing was ever going right.

I'd look at some new mums (especially on Instagram) and think, *Are you getting fully glammed up for the photos, then spending the next twenty-three and a half hours crying? Or are you genuinely finding it easy?* I think if you're an influencer with millions of followers, you have a responsibility to be open and honest with the people listening to you if you're not finding it a breeze, particularly in those early days of motherhood, when now more than 1 in 10 women are affected by PND, not to mention their partners who can also suffer from it – and some research has shown that lockdown made PND twice as likely. I believe that those expecting should know that they might love motherhood, but they also might hate it, and that's normal too. And if that's you, then there's support and help you can get. You might not get on with every aspect of parenting, but talking about it with the right people can make a massive difference to how you feel each day.

I think a shift is happening. I've seen Instagrammers starting to be more open about the struggles they're having, the changes their bodies have made, the mess their homes are in, the medication they're taking to help themselves and their babies. I look at the photos of me in those first months, greasy mum bun, wearing nothing but white granny pants and a dressing gown with eye bags for days, my face is just one big eye-bag, but I wanted to speak as much as possible about a truth I gradually discovered wasn't mine alone.

And who knows? Maybe it actually isn't all sunshine and rainbows for some couples. Or maybe I'm just hugely envious when it is. I wouldn't wish the feelings I had on anyone in the world, but it never stopped me feeling like I'd been hit in the stomach when another happy mum posed with her calm and happy baby for the 'Gram. Is it lacking in sensitivity for happy mums to talk a lot about how easy and joyful they're finding it? Or am I oversensitive for being upset by it? Like I say, I'd never stop anyone, but it's one of the reasons I never post a picture of my mum or Noa on Mother's Day each year. My mum knows I love her, and I don't need to post pictures on social media to prove that to anyone, or to prove my bond with Noa – but there are women out there whose mothers have passed, who don't speak to their mothers, who would love to be mothers but aren't, who have just had gone through pregnancy loss, or those who don't ever want to be a mother, and I'd rather send them some love that day than post a perfect shot of any personal happiness I'm experiencing.

9

Silver Linings

I don't remember waking up one morning and thinking, *Oh, I feel great today, everything's OK again!* But my body and my mind gradually began to feel better as Siobhan came in, I was having regular therapy with Anna, my boss told me to take more maternity leave, and lockdown restrictions were slowly being lifted so people were able to come over. The day I stopped breastfeeding, too, it felt like the biggest weight had gone. I felt sad that those days of skin-to-skin closeness with Noa were over, but I had a sense of freedom: I could go out, I could have a drink – as a side note, totally fine to have the odd drink when breastfeeding – have fun, get some Botox (that's when I discovered Botox is now wasted on me). Boj could help with night feeds and I knew I could give Noa a full feed without her crying on my boobs. I knew she was getting enough and putting on weight.

It was a real turning point. I still had bad days, but they were fewer, and they were easier to cope with. And at five months we also moved Noa into her own room. The NHS recommends your baby sleeps in your room until they're six months old, but our bedroom was so light and hers had a blackout blind, plus we had a baby monitor that came with a sock she wore every night that tracked her heart rate and oxygen levels and showed the stats via the app on my phone. It meant I could sleep that bit better.

I'd been given a prescription for antidepressants after a friend had said how much they'd helped her in her first year, but I was hesitant about taking them and wanted to see if giving up alcohol for a month and trying something more natural would improve my feelings of sadness. The feelings had returned when Noa was around seven months, at the point Boj had fully returned to work and the end of my maternity leave was approaching, which re-sparked my anxiety. I'd started to drink more alcohol, and I could see it was having a negative impact on my mental health, then I would start worrying about what the anxiety was doing to my body long-term and whether it was damaging my heart, so I quit the booze and began taking a few drops of CBD oil instead in the morning and evening. I immediately slept better, and felt happier and less anxious.

But that wasn't the end of it – with mental health, it never is . . .

And never mind being grateful that Boj stayed with me through the third trimester – I'm amazed that he's still here after everything that came after. I know I'm not to blame for my PND, but I also know living with someone suffering from depression is hard, and Boj was always so supportive and patient when all I could think was that I was dragging him down. I couldn't stop thinking, *Why is he still with me? How can he want to be here when all I do is moan and cry?* And that became a real issue. Eventually, he suggested couples' therapy because he knew we were struggling and wanted to work through our problems in order for us to stay together, and get into the best habits we could as we started the next chapter of our life together. When Boj first suggested it, though, it sent me spiralling, and I thought this was the start of him breaking up with me. I also didn't think I could talk to a stranger about any relationship issues I had, but it's actually helped me be more honest and upfront with Boj. Talking to him and to our therapist Diana, and to other friends who have gone through couples' therapy, made me see it totally differently: it was a sign of a healthy relationship that we wanted to work at it, and find an opportunity to listen to each other, even if it was nerve-wracking and awkward to begin with. Even though we've been together eight years, there's still so much I struggle to articulate at times; I would rather just shut myself away and not deal with it, not bring it up and hope that any problem goes away, but I don't want Noa growing up with parents who do that. And maybe we wouldn't be doing this if we didn't have Noa, so that's another positive she's brought to our lives, pushing us to make our relationship as strong and healthy as possible. It's not always easy, but it's definitely the right thing to do.

If there's one piece of advice I would give to partners, it would be to step up and appreciate how much work goes into mothering a newborn, because it is often left so much to the mum. Whatever type of relationship you're in, a lot of partners feel like they don't know what to do or that they're less involved, but you just need to be there every day, asking what the mum needs and helping without being asked. If she's feeding, make her food and a drink as well, put a wash on, unload the dishwasher, run her a bath and offer to have the baby for half an hour while she can wash and relax, or take the baby for a walk so she can sleep. I can't tell you how much these little gestures will make her feel better. If you can divide things like nappy changes and feeds as equally as possible, you'll both get a bit of time to shower or make a coffee or nap for ten minutes. You're both going to be tired and saying things you might not mean, but it's about accepting the state you're in and drawing a fresh line each night. Point-scoring doesn't help anyone, and it's just one more thing to be dealing with that really doesn't need to happen. It helps to have a sense of humour, too. When I'm asking Boj to do stuff now, he just says, 'Yes, boss. No, boss.' He can't be bothered to argue when I'm being ridiculous, but something about the way he says it always makes me laugh – instead of having an argument, we both just end up laughing together.

From the start, it's been really important that Boj and I do equal parenting – he always said that if we had a baby, it would be 50/50, and so far we've managed that a lot of the time. Sometimes we share it out, and sometimes we do it together, but we try to make it so no one is ever doing more than half of everything. I'm glad he's a man of his word, and it means we have time to ourselves to do things on our own, and we can come back refreshed to spend time all together and enjoy it.

Sex has obviously changed so much from the pre-baby days. Because I got pregnant so quickly, we thankfully never got to that stage where sex was a chore, or to the point where I'd be chasing him around the flat at a particularly fertile time each month, or doing it way more than either of us actually wanted to, which let's face it, isn't every night. This made a big difference, but even so I was surprised during pregnancy how much we were doing it. It was only quite late in my third trimester, when my bump was so big and I felt so unattractive, that it just felt weird. I said, 'I think we're just going to have to say goodbye to sex until she's out.' I know friends who have had really different reactions to sex during pregnancy: one friend couldn't bear the thought of sex from the day she found out she was pregnant to about six months after the baby was born, and another friend's boyfriend was the same, just very weirded out by it. On the other hand, a different friend's husband had a massive thing for pregnancy and found her the sexiest ever. It just depends on your preference, I suppose.

After Noa was born, we had to wait for my check-up to see if anything was infected or needed further care, but afterwards when we did start trying to have sex again, I found it pretty difficult. Both physically and emotionally, even though I hadn't given birth to Noa through my vagina, that whole thing felt pretty closed for business. It was almost four months before we had sex again, and longer still before we worked out how to make it work for us. Now we'll have a bit of morning fun while she's napping – in the evening we're usually far too tired. I've never been a 9.30 in the morning kind of girl, a 'Let's go, we've got fifteen minutes' type of person, but I'd rather have sex I'm enjoying, even if it's at an odd time, and countless guests on our podcast have reminded us of the importance of keeping the spark going as a couple. My body isn't exactly the same as before, but that's OK too: if I don't feel as attractive as I used to, I know I just need to make a bit more of an effort, get a spray tan, have a manicure, go to the gym or blow-dry and curl my hair (I don't remember the last time I did all those things). Exercise used to be such a massive part of my life, but at first I was frightened of my scar opening up, and then I just got out of the habit, but I do want to feel like my body is mine again. I know how good I can feel with sex and exercise. I'm just pleased that Boj and I still like each other, we still want each other, and we're still making the time for each other.

It was never like a switch had flicked, but those moments of light, which seemed so occasional, became more frequent. One night I was up with Noa I did a Q&A on Instagram about what other women had nicknamed their boobs (mine had long since become Phil and Grant, after the big, bald Albert Square hard men they resembled after my milk came in. Phil sadly became less reliable, so I ended up feeding Noa exclusively from Grant in her last month of breastfeeding). My faves:

- Fearne & Holly
- Ant & Dec (because one's bigger than the other)

- Flip & Flop
- Bill & Ted
- Chaz & Dave
- Dolce & Gabbana
- Ronnie & Reggie (I mean, WTF?)
- Britney & Whitney
- Thelma & Louise
- Doris & Derrick ('My double Ds')

The responses made me laugh so much, it was a welcome distraction from the tears that rolled daily. My other favourite Q&A was when I asked other parents what lengths they had gone to in order to not disturb their baby, after I was in the disgusting position of having to let snot run down my face as I had nothing to blow my nose with and sniffing made Noa jump. These still make me cry laughing now:

- My partner gets hay fever so I make him sneeze into the pillow so he doesn't wake the baby
- I didn't flush the toilet at night for three years
- Sat on a hotel bathroom floor eating McDonald's chicken nuggets
- Pissed myself so I didn't have to move her. Luckily, I had a Tena Lady on.
- Made my husband wee onto the bowl instead of into the water as it was too loud

- Played Scrabble in complete silence
- Peed in a vase at my mum's house, as walking to the bathroom would wake her because of the creaky floorboards
- Peed in the garden so I didn't have to walk past my daughter's bedroom
- Silent arguments – lots of hand gestures and Britney lip sync
- Drank wine with my mate in the utility room so as not to wake my baby asleep in the living room
- Held two nappies underneath my crotch and peed while holding my sixteen month old as I couldn't put her down
- Army-crawled out of the room on my hands and knees
- Watched an entire movie on mute with subtitles
- Played the *Guardians of the Galaxy Volume 1* soundtrack through the baby monitor – it was the only way I could leave the room without him noticing and waking up
- Put small glow-in-the-dark stickers on the creaky bits of the floor so I don't walk on them
- Got a latex glove, filled it with sand and laid it on the baby so she thought I was stood with my hand on her
- Held a shit in for approximately four hours

It's amazing what we think is a rational choice when we're that tired. And it's staggering how we think the human race has lasted this long, too, if a creaky floorboard or the sound of a Scrabble tile would be so disastrous.

The diagnosis of GAD, generalised anxiety disorder, really came out when I started thinking about leaving Noa with someone else. Even if it was with close family members, even with Boj, I just had this overwhelming fear of something terrible happening to her, of her choking or suffocating and dying, and I couldn't handle it at all. When I spoke to Anna about it in therapy, she said, 'You have to leave her before you go back to work. Start by leaving her for an hour with Boj's mum while you two go for a coffee, and build up from there.' The shock of leaving her for five hours plus when I went back to work would have had me quitting my job on the first day if I hadn't taken Anna's advice, even though the first time we tried I only managed to stay away for forty minutes. The next week, I made a big leap, leaving Noa with Boj's mum and arranging to meet a friend for lunch a thirty-minute drive away. Noa was in a good routine by then, and the timings meant she'd just need a bottle and a nap. Easy.

Unfortunately, I'd put the baby monitor on my phone, and could only watch from miles away at the restaurant table as Noa howled in the cot, and Boj's mum did her best to soothe her, but I could tell it wasn't working, and Sue didn't pick up the phone because she was trying to calm the baby. From that distance, and with all the guilt and panic screaming in my body, I couldn't remember that she had successfully raised two children, and that Noa wasn't in any danger. Instead, I panicked, rang Boj sobbing hysterically, and left my lunch to drive straight home – it's a miracle I didn't have some kind of crash. That day was a total disaster, and I needed to go back several steps and rebuild my confidence. We put a big sheet of paper up on the fridge with all the issues that might arise, and how any babysitter was supposed to deal with it, and I did more and more short trips out, until it was time to go back to work and I felt totally fine with trusting that Noa would be OK if I left her for a day.

(I'm not always perfect at it – we did spend our most recent anniversary at a very nice fancy restaurant where I kept checking in on Noa, who was fast asleep, via the monitor app on my phone, but I'm definitely improving.)

In terms of going back to work, take off as much time as you possibly can. Twelve weeks seemed like ages when I asked for it – a nice long holiday is two weeks, so twelve would be *ages*, she'd be in a routine and everything will be easy by then. Oh yeah, remember also when I'd given myself twelve weeks to be ready for our wedding? *Mad.* Even at six weeks, I suddenly realised: how can I possibly leave her in six more weeks? But my boss had a lot more sense than me, and had also seen some of the things I was posting on Instagram. He got in touch and offered me much more time, which I gladly took. I wasn't anywhere near ready to go back then, not physically, mentally, or emotionally. Don't feel pressure to go back before you're ready, because the most important thing is your baby, and you are not replaceable as a mother, but someone can come and do your job at work for a bit longer. If you've got the opportunity to be at home at the start, do it. Around eight months worked for me, then I went back part-time – you need to just be in a state where you're confident about leaving your baby, and your baby is secure in a routine, and you know that you'll come back and everything will still be OK. It's also worth looking into how you could potentially split parental leave with any partner, and how that could work for your family emotionally and financially.

It was great that Anna prepped me for work by having me leave Noa for those hours I'd be away. It meant that when I did go back, I could really enjoy being in that adult world again, having fun with my colleagues and doing my work well. Of course, I still miss her, still want photos and videos of her while I'm working, but I'm no longer frightened, or anxious, and I can just have a laugh being Kate Lawler, DJ, not Kate-mum-of-Noa.

I feel like I've got a different kind of purpose at Virgin Radio, playing music and talking, and that's a fantastic feeling that allows me to function as an adult, not only as a mum – if you're lucky enough to enjoy your work, there's a real value in going back to it.

And it meant that one day after my first couple of weeks back, I had a full day with Noa, and when Boj came home I was really excited to tell him all the stuff we'd done. 'We went swimming, we've had such a laugh, we've been out with the dogs, we've had the best day!'

He looked at me for a moment, then said, 'You've never said that before. You've never said you've had a great day with her.' So we marked it down, eight and a half months was when I could finally have a full day with Noa without getting upset, and I could also actually *enjoy* it. After all those people had said, 'Get through three months, four months, six months,' it was at eight and a half months that I really, really began loving having that time with her.

I know how much I'll miss Noa if I go away for the night, but I'm also looking forward to it, whenever that day might be. We talked in one episode of our podcast about how important it is to have time away from your children, so you can miss them and have the space to be excited about seeing them again. Although I took almost nine months off work, it wasn't remotely a break.

When you're actually doing parental leave, it's clear that you're not taking time off, you're just doing a different job: raising a child (a job that doesn't have holidays, rest breaks, or even a reasonable boss). I love my job, I'm incredibly lucky to do it, and the intimacy of radio is amazing, knowing you're keeping all kinds of people company – whether they're at home, at work, on the road – and with one little anecdote or joke, you might just be cheering up someone who's had a really bad day. But work–life balance is so important. Whether it's for kids, or a hobby, or just to have some headspace, it's better for employers to have workers who are healthy, functioning people, rather than just working them into the ground. I want to spend as much time with Noa as I can before she starts school, because that time will fly, I know, but I also need to have time doing something professional to keep my brain happy and active. But I get home late from work three nights a week now, which means by the time she wakes up in the morning I've not seen her for eighteen hours, and I am *so* excited to see her. Her face lights up with the biggest smile as I walk into her nursery and she sees me, as though it's been eighteen months instead of hours. I can't imagine what I'll be like when she's too old to miss me back.

At least the dogs will always greet me like their long-lost very-best friend.

A word with . . . Siobhan
(our post-natal doula/night nanny)

I've been a doula for eleven years, preparing mothers for birth and offering continuity of care all the way through, supporting them emotionally and practically up to and including the birth, and with post-natal care too. I'd had my three children before I'd even heard about doulas; my first labour was very medicalised, but the second time around I was a bit more informed and able to make decisions. My third was completely spontaneous, and it was only that time that I thought, *I get what I'm doing now.* I had thought ignorance was bliss, but actually all those medical interventions that I was uninformed about led to complications and post-natal issues for my first baby. The role of a doula is about empowering women to get the right birth for them on the day – we know there's no one right way of birthing.

Being a doula involves being able to read people and be empathetic to their needs. You're going into their space when they're at their most vulnerable, and just being present to support them however they need. Sometimes it's the mum who needs help, and other times we're there to support the partner so they can support the mum – it's about what makes the family happier as a whole, working with them as a team. Research shows that having a doula reduces the need for instrumental delivery, significantly lowers the rates of caesarean, and allows much higher rates of breastfeeding, all of which will help the mum, the baby, and any other family members.

Often we'll be booked around their twenty-week scan, but sometimes, like with Kate, we'll be called in post-birth when things might be really difficult. We can be there to give them the time to talk and be honest about how they're feeling, and provide them with the information to know what is actually normal. So many unrealistic expectations come from social media, and books written by people who don't truly understand the needs of a baby; there's a lot of emotional advice, anecdotal advice, rather than evidence-based information that is safe and will work to address the needs of the baby, who has gone from being rocked for nine months in the dark, cosy

environment of the womb to being put flat on
their back in a cold cot. No wonder they don't
settle! There are tips and tricks that can help to
transition a baby down into a crib to give you
a few minutes, because we recognise that as a
parent, you do need to have a shower, you need
to just have a bit of space, and we're not there to
judge you on your decisions, but to support you.
People are a bit guarded with someone like a
health visitor, worried that if they say they aren't
happy, will social services be sent in? Are they
going to report me to somebody? Doulas are there
to say, 'Whatever help you need, we've been there,
we get it.'

We can signpost people to the best-quality
research about safe sleeping, feeding, caring, so
they can make an informed decision when they're
otherwise in a very vulnerable, fragile state. A
lot of 'advice' parents get is just belief-based,
and it should be evidence-based and completely
non-biased. The biggest struggle for parents is
the baby's sleep. There's this misconception that
everybody should be hell-bent on getting their
babies to sleep, but babies aren't meant to sleep

longer. They have tiny stomachs and can only eat small quantities, so they're not designed to go into very deep sleep: they're light sleepers that need to be fed often. More antenatal care early on should prepare people for that period when babies are not designed to sleep through long periods.

Even as adults, we don't sleep through the night. If we are uncomfortable, we can turn ourselves over, we can flip the pillow onto the cold side, scoop the duvet off, reach for a little drink. Babies can't do any of that, so they have to wake themselves up and signal that they need some help, and that's by crying. Those early months are about having realistic expectations by understanding the physiological cause of your baby doing certain things; they do those things for a reason, to survive, and understanding those reasons can help us as parents meet their needs. But to do all that, parents need support, so it's a team effort.

Informed is always best. Breastfeeding is such an emotive subject, but it's the system that lets us down at every turn. There's no money to be made from breastfeeding, so there's no systemic support. When it comes to breastfeeding, a doula's role is to listen to the mum: what does she need? What would she like to achieve in the next week, day, hour? And then supporting her and her choice, from how she feeds to when she might stop breastfeeding. Where mums are supported by doulas or in areas with good breastfeeding support, the rates speak for themselves, but you need good information, good family support and good community support.

How much do pregnant women get told about hormones, for example, and how initial breastfeeding requires the correct set of hormones to be working freely? Oxytocin, for example, is very heightened in birth, and you need that relaxed state, feeling completely comfortable, to successfully feed. If you've got streams of visitors and you're having to sit upstairs on your own with the baby because you don't want to be trying to feed in front of your father-in-law, it will be much harder, emotionally *and* physiologically. Those women that feel they've failed at breastfeeding – they haven't. The system has failed them. We need a huge injection of capital into the maternity systems, into women's health in general.

When we came to Kate and Boj, they looked the way a lot of first-time parents look at that stage: like rabbits in the headlights. And of course, Noa had a lot of things going on in those early days, and a lot of antibiotics that affected her gut. From what I observed, I thought there may possibly be some kind of jaw tension and tongue-tie issue, so I mentioned that to Kate and gave her the number of a tongue-tie specialist – it's just signposting, giving parents an option and allowing them to build up confidence in good information and their own abilities.

There's no such thing as a bad parent, only bad support. No one brings a child into the world not wanting to care for them, but it does take a village to raise a child. Most people would stay where they grew up, in previous times, and be surrounded by friends and cousins and relatives, but now I work with a lot of professionals who can command a boardroom, but because they commute in to work, they know absolutely no one in their area. It can be very lonely, and that early support is vital.

Knowing that at two o'clock in the morning

when you can't console your baby, the phone pings and there's someone there saying, 'Yeah, I'm the same.' You know it's not just you, that you're not doing anything wrong.

My advice for anyone considering having a baby is to get a doula, and get yourself good antenatal education to understand the physiology behind birth and what's required to allow your body to birth your baby. We're designed to birth our babies. We've been doing it for a long time. What we need to do is trust the process. We have the medical side there, thank God, and when it's needed, you couldn't be in better hands than the NHS. But if everything is OK with birth, it really should be undisturbed.

Doula care is much more accessible than people might think. There are always doulas at various stages of their training and experience, so there will be a sliding scale of costs, and most doulas offer payment plans or gift vouchers, so instead of a collection of teddy bears that will sit on a shelf, friends can chip in for a post-natal doula. For vulnerable women, there's the PIF Programme, which anyone can donate to, for survivors of trafficking or domestic abuse, asylum seekers, prisoners, anybody on a very low income, so they can access that care free of charge.

Watching Kate and Boj with Noa, it's clear they're so in tune with her and always meet her needs. She's a very happy baby, and very confident. She knows that if she needs something, her parents will sort it out. They just need to keep doing what they're doing.

10

Growing Up

Once we started to feel like we had a handle on Noa's basic routine (sleeping and feeding), of course she only went and got older. She was changing every day, babbling and rolling over, but also changing her sleep patterns as she needed more food – so weaning began. She had the dummy, too, which she only used for sleeping, but someone gave us the very good advice that it's easier to train away a dummy for a baby than it is to try and negotiate away the dummy with a three-year-old, after spending years worrying about lost dummies in the car, on a train, on a day out. I couldn't handle the thought of that *at all*. My friend Rosey, a sleep consultant, advised us to remove the dummy for the very first time at night, rather than before a day nap, so Noa was extra tired and ready to go down easier – Noa was already at the stage where at night she'd wake up, find her dummy and be holding it, but she couldn't quite work out how to put it back in her mouth, so she'd wake us up crying and eventually the hourly dummy runs became too much.

The first night, I fed her, tucked her up and gave her a small, soft, wool comfy she likes to nuzzle into, and she looked a bit confused, like, thanks for my comfy but *where's the dummy?* I gave her a kiss and left the room. After a couple of minutes she began to get really upset and I couldn't bear to do the 'cry it out' method, so I went back in and cuddled her, but she was hysterical. After around half an hour she calmed down and fell asleep in my arms. I felt terrible but I had to remind myself: short-term pain, long-term gain. Rocking her to sleep and telling her it was all going to be OK made me feel less guilty than leaving her to cry, but I wondered if I'd just created a new habit to replace the dummy one. However, the next night she only took fifteen minutes to settle without the dummy, and slept until four a.m. After a quick nappy change I put her gently down again, thinking she'd not go back to sleep without her dummy, but she proved me wrong and the night after that she slept until five a.m. The whole thing took about a week, and she was a bit confused and upset when it came to certain naps, but we'd built up enough confidence and calm that I could get through it without feeling I was doing something terrible to Noa. The comfy is a lifesaver, though – in our day, I remember having an old piece of rag that came from a terry towelling nappy, but fast forward forty years and babies are now cosying up to beautiful comforters with toys and ribbon labels on to play with. So Noa has her beautiful comfy that she snuggles up to and puts herself right to sleep. It's a miracle. We are very lucky parents.

I feel like children consistently lull you into a false sense of security: you think you know their habits and routines, so you relax, and then they show you that you have absolutely no control at all. We went to see my friend in Manchester last year, on what should have been a really simple train trip; me, Noa, Boj, and the dogs. Noa had been in a perfect routine for months, we'd packed really lightly on the advice of the friend we were visiting who already had loads of equipment, and we'd booked the train so she could feed, then have her morning nap on the way there.

Of course, she was having none of it. Cried almost the entire journey until a number of passengers left the carriage to go find some peace and quiet. (It didn't help that for some reason I hadn't booked seats at a table, just two backward-facing seats – how were the five of us meant to manage? What were we thinking?) Then she didn't bother to have any naps or to sleep properly that night or the next day. On the way back we paid the extra £25 each to go into First Class in order to have more space and, unlike the previous day, it was the least stressful journey. The train carriage was empty, and we made it back with no drama, but it did make our minds up that we wouldn't be doing that again in a hurry. For now if people want to see us, they are always welcome and we love hosting, but the stress of the train and trying to get Noa to sleep somewhere new just brought all those feelings back that I don't cope well with, that everyone is watching me, judging me as a mum and knowing I'm not doing a very good job. Of course, people watching are probably really sympathetic, and I probably look like I'm doing OK. But when Noa is screaming, I get that sense again that I'm letting her down, and it wears me away inside. It does mean now that even though I still don't consider myself maternal, if I saw a woman struggling with a crying baby on a plane or something, I'd offer to take the baby for a walk up the aisle. I would never have done that when I was younger, before Noa, but I can see how just giving her a few minutes and letting her know that the whole plane isn't against her, can be a huge help.

The train journey is a really good symbol of how things have changed over the years for me. When I was in my thirties, the train meant just me and Baxter, who'd always be given a sausage from the train staff while I sat and read a magazine. Then Boj came along, then Shirley, then Noa, and now train journeys are a whole new ball game, they're stressful and sweaty, and we have both way too much stuff and too little stuff, and I need to lie down in a quiet room afterwards, and if we do take a good photo it's pure luck of timing, a snapshot of smiles amid the chaotic and tense two-hour journey.

Not that I want to wish the early years away but I'm actually looking forward to doing this kind of stuff once she's old enough to eat a sandwich, wipe her own bum, read a book on the train, and not have to nap twice a day. There are five of us in our pack, and five is a pretty stressful number even on the best days. I think we all need to manage our expectations and not be comparing ourselves to those who seem to be living a practically perfect life, going out all the time, everyone dressed in beautiful clothes, visiting amazing places. If you can only manage one thing this week, that's fine! There's so many ways to spend time as a family without it having to be what you *think* is right, rather than what actually makes you all happy.

Now that we have Noa, we get invitations from friends to join them on family trips away. Although it's lovely to be invited, I have *no* interest in going on holiday with multiple families where children outnumber the adults. We love our friends, but again I'm still at the point where I know I won't cope if Noa has a meltdown in the middle of a nice day out, or where she might be unsettled at night because she's away from all the things that make her feel happy, and I'm still not a fan of being surrounded by lots of children and watching my best friends in parent mode. In my closest group of friends we have twenty-three kids between us. They range from newborns to twenty-one-year-olds, and they often do day trips or weekends away together. My parents did the same when we were children and I've really fond memories of hanging out all the time with the children of Mum and Dad's best friends. My mates will say, 'Come! You can bring Noa!' And perhaps this is where I'm still struggling to accept that I'm a parent now and this is what mums and dads do, but I politely decline. I want to hang out with my friends when we don't have our babies, when we can have a proper catch-up and a glass of wine, and not have to keep half an eye out for our kids. I want to go on holiday with my girlfriends or just Boj, Noa and the doggies. Going away in a huge group just doesn't feel like a holiday to me.

On the 'MILF Chat', our WhatsApp group, they insist it will be heaps of fun, with zoo trips and swimming pools and caravans, but I just can't bring myself to say yes because right now a weekend with Noa anywhere that isn't her bed feels like it's going to be too much. My anxiety gets the better of me. I wish I could say every time we've been away with her has been sunshine and rainbows, but it's been terribly full-on and more tiring than anything. When she's older, I know we'll all really enjoy these kind of trips – when she can recognise the other kids and get excited about seeing them, but at her current age, I personally find it stressful enough just with one child, let alone twenty-three of them.

But I've also made some really good friends through having Noa. We'd always have spent time with our lovely neighbours, but the fact that we all have children roughly the same ages means we hang out a lot more. I met another woman totally randomly, a local mum, and we now go for walks together with our babies and dogs, and there have been other women I've met through Instagram and then bonded with in real life. Mostly it's been great to meet new people like that, but occasionally, like when a friend of a friend gives me the eye-roll for not registering Noa at a nursery before she was even conceived, I just have to shove more pain au raisin into my mouth to stop myself saying something I'd regret. (I mean, that is something I wish I'd listened to: *put their names down for nursery when they're born*. Even if you don't know when you'll go back to work, or exactly what days you'll do, just get their name down. I remember Siobhan, the night nanny, saying when Noa was about six weeks old, 'You should get her registered at a nursery.' I thought that was a daft idea, she was barely out of my tummy, but she said, 'I'm telling you – get her name down.' Yeah, no spaces when she was turning one and we needed it. Don't make the same mistake as me.)

My twin, Karen, still comes weekly as our cleaner – although really it's an excuse to see Noa, I reckon – and I definitely feel closer to my mum now. I've always been a daddy's girl, but Mum was so happy and supportive when Noa was coming that it's brought us much closer. The fact that my brother is the only other one with a girl in the family has meant his girlfriend and I have got much closer too. It's been great keeping in touch with some of the guests we've had on the podcast as well – Ellie Taylor has been a lifesaver sometimes, talking about how she got through that first difficult year as a mum. Anna Whitehouse and I met up too, and she had so much wonderful advice.

So, with the wisdom from these other mums, and with a year of Noa under our belt, these are two key aspects you might want to know about when dealing with a baby yourself . . .

SLEEPING

When it comes to sleep, I wish I'd enjoyed those new-born cuddles a bit more, and let her fall asleep on me without worrying. There's absolutely no point trying to force a routine on a newborn because they're not robots. A friend of mine, from day one of Noa being born, kept trying to get us on a schedule, which seemed totally mad to me even then. Just follow your baby's lead for at least the first six to eight weeks – it was around this time we began an evening routine. Find ways to make them comfortable and safe, and get enough rest so you can respond to their needs, but otherwise, they'll tell you when they want to feed and sleep.

A good friend asked me if I wanted to know how she'd got her girls sleeping 7 p.m. to 7 a.m. every night by twelve weeks. You might think it's all down to sheer luck, but she talked me through their routine: give them a bath every night at the same time, then a nice little body massage, then a fresh nappy, clean vest and baby-gro, and into a dark, quiet room for the bedtime feed. Feed her, cuddle her, and put her in her bed.

We had nothing to lose by trying it, so we started by giving Noa a bath and bringing her downstairs, feeding her with the lights dimmed and TV volume low, so she gradually picked up the difference between day and night, which helped her develop her circadian rhythm; getting to learn when the time was we'd chat and play and sing with her, and when it was time for resting and quiet. We didn't want to force her into any rigid schedules, but just moving the Moses basket she was in from our kitchen snug to the dining room (with the monitor on) while we ate dinner in the kitchen and watched a bit of TV was great for two reasons: one – Boj and I got to finally spend a couple of hours alone in the evening, and two – Noa was gradually sleeping a bit longer each night in a darker, more quiet room. We'd take her in the Moses basket up to our room when it was time for bed and if she woke up needing changing, feeding or just a kiss and a cuddle, we'd be there for her. I believe she got so comfortable with her evening bath, feed and sleep routine that it made her the good sleeper that she is right now. Of course, every baby is different, and every baby will be on a different rhythm, but this meant Noa could find her own pattern, gradually dropping night feeds as the weeks went on and she could sleep for longer.

It's also worth noting that Moses baskets are great because they're moveable, but also they are so much smaller than a crib or cot, so the baby isn't in this vast, airy space. In the Moses basket we could put Noa in her swaddle where she looked so cosy and began to sleep really well; Siobhan recommended something called the Love to Dream Swaddle Up, which is a swaddle with an unusual design, keeping the baby's hands up near its face, which is how young babies prefer to sleep (rather than having arms and hands pinned down by their sides or tight to their chest). Noa was too much of a wriggler for the traditional swaddle, but this looked so soothing, and really cute – you just zip them into the swaddle up bag, and they look like a little angel with wings, or a glowworm. As the baby gets older, they move from that to a bag with removable arms, then to a sleeping bag, and every one of those has been just great for Noa. Siobhan also showed us how to put Noa down into the basket, leaning in with her really slowly and keeping our bodies close to her so she could still hear and smell and sense us, that she wasn't just being dumped and left in her sleep space. The dummy also helped, and because we only gave it to her after a few weeks she never got that hooked on it, just associated it naturally with sleep time, rather than a self-comforting thing all day that may have made it harder to get rid of. It does soothe babies, so don't feel guilty about using one. That's what it's for.

And I stand by my advice for resting: if you can't sleep when your baby sleeps – because who knows? The baby might fall asleep just after you've downed a triple-shot macchiato – just give yourself some quiet time. No housework, no replying to work emails, no urgent errands. Just put your feet up, have a cup of tea, relax, and take the pressure off yourself. You need the rest to function as a mum, and as a person. Another tip I discovered too late was to give yourself nights off, if you can. One of my friends would, once a week, go into the spare room, put earplugs in and an eye mask on, and her partner did all the night feeds so she could get a full night's sleep. That might not work for you for any number of reasons, but even as a one-off it's worth the chance to recharge your batteries and reset, because so often everything is easier after a good night's sleep.

Of course, it wasn't a perfectly smooth line of sleep progress: at eight months Noa suddenly started waking at six a.m. instead of seven, so I got in touch with Rosey, the sleep consultant, who suggested I move her morning nap back fifteen minutes, from 9.15 to 9.30. And it worked! That's magic, and something I would never have thought of myself in a million years. She was also the one who suggested I turn the baby monitor volume off at around eight months – we were in the next room with open doors, able to hear her every move, yet I had this speaker next to me waking me every time Noa would wriggle or make a little sound or whine. By now Noa wasn't ever in distress or hungry, she was just momentarily waking up before dropping off again, and I would have woken her up if I'd gone in, but it took Rosey saying that for me to turn the sound off and get a decent night's sleep. Game changer.

WEANING

I'm not a food person. I mean, eating it? Yes. Making it? Not so much.

Weaning is one of those areas where absolutely everyone has an opinion, and can't wait to share it with you. The best advice came from Siobhan, our night nanny, who said we could tell when to begin weaning Noa because she'd start staring at the food going into our mouths as we were eating, and start to try and grab at the food. As soon as that happened, we were ready.

Boj and I were lucky enough to go and see Annabel Karmel, the weaning queen, and actually go to her house. She has a stunning home, with the longest kitchen island I've ever seen, in fact the dream kitchen, multiple ovens, and a huge fish tank, which hypnotised Noa completely. It was only when we got there that we realised we'd turned up without Noa's bottle and she was due a feed – absolute bloody amateurs – but the three of us managed not to humiliate ourselves, and went home with Annabel's books, and a few weeks after that Boj was making the most amazing food from her recipes, not only for Noa but bigger versions for us too. Boj is a true chef, and he made all sorts of delicious stuff like tofu burgers, lentil soup and fish in cornflakes because he loves watching us eat and enjoying something he's made. He was a big fan of batch cooking for Noa then freezing the food in ice cube trays, then when it was Noa's mealtime, we'd just pop three or four ice cubes in her food bowl and defrost them for her lunch or dinner. If Boj didn't cook I'd have been giving Noa pouches 24/7. Sometimes when there was nothing left in the freezer, or we were out and about, we'd give her a pouch which she loved – it's all fresh fruit and veg, even if I can't work out how the hell it stays fresh for months on end. Seriously, how can a pouch with *just* strawberries in not start to smell when it's been stored in a kitchen cupboard for months on end? I never want food to become an issue in our house; I just want it to be something Noa can enjoy, and we can all share together.

As soon as she could sit up, at around five and a half months, she had purees, and *loved* them. You could see her thinking, *Something other than milk, thank goodness!* She loved sweet potato (probably because she's our sweet Tayto), butternut squash and veggies. She loved the green smoothie Boj makes us, which looks like the

Bog of Eternal Stench but she'd kick her legs and coo madly for it. I got a bit nervous at first about her choking, so we stayed on purees for ages (producing the most disgusting massive nappies, which Boj would somehow always disappear for), then I worried about how much food she would eat – or not eat – and whether she was still getting enough milk, and of course there were plenty of people asking, 'Why aren't you doing baby-led weaning?' which made me doubt everything we were doing. Of course the answer, as with all things about your baby, was 'Because this is what works for us,' but I chilled out because I could see how much Noa was enjoying the experience, always making these beautiful little *hmmm mm hmmmm* noises when she tries something she really likes, copying the 'Yum yum yum' noise I make when I feed her and smacking her lips together after a bite like I taught her to do.

For breakfast, she loved pikelets, those little thin crumpets, or porridge, or scrambled eggs. We just rotated those, plus the smoothies if we were having them, then for lunch Boj would batchcook salt-free recipes, and then before we knew it she was just eating whatever we ate. I would still always panic a bit when she gagged, seeing her face go red and her eyes water but I had to remind myself it was perfectly normal and it meant her reflex was dealing with the food. Watching her once try and stuff a massive bit of Turkish flatbread into her mouth sent me having to scoop the whole thing out of her mouth with my finger after she gave me an accusing look and started to gag. I still worry about things like grapes and blueberries, which can be choking risks up to the age of five, but I really enjoy eating with her and watching her try new foods. As long as we can keep trying them together, that's what matters.

Fed in the day and in bed at night, and you'll hopefully be enjoying your baby by the end of the first year too. Then you'll have all those firsts to look forward to . . .

II

The Big Firsts

Part of the joy of a baby is meant to be all their firsts. Well, I can tell you that for all Noa's firsts, some have been wonderful, some have been disastrous, but they've all been . . . memorable.

FIRST CLOTHING DISASTER

Our first trip to the pub was memorable for the contrast between Noa's fresh appearance at the start of the visit (gleaming white babygro ready for her to fall asleep) and her finished look, where I'd been holding her and not realised chipotle sauce was dripping out of my burger and onto my daughter, which made her and Boj both laugh.

Long before that, however, when Noa was suffering

with terrible reflux, Siobhan recommended a cranial osteopath we might want to try. Boj encouraged me to go alone and see how I went – the clinic was only just down the road from us, so we wouldn't be too far away. On a scorching afternoon, I drove down with Noa, out for the first time on my own, and parked outside the clinic, much too early for our appointment but pleased I'd got us out of the house and on time. I thought, *We've got so much time, I'll just check in case she needs a change.* As soon as I turned the engine off, the car was like a sauna, but I got into the back and I lifted her out of the car seat. Yes, she definitely needed a change. She was still so tiny, just weeks old, so I put the mat down on the back seat and lifted up what she was wearing to reveal . . . an *explosion*. It was at that moment that I realised: I didn't have spare clothes for her. Or wipes. And as I watched, more started to come out, and it went *everywhere.*

It's difficult to describe something like that if you haven't witnessed it yourself. This wee-poo mixture that suddenly was all over everything, all over me, all over her, the back seats, her car seat, all the while the temperature rising in the car. I was gagging and retching, trying to wipe her down with her dirty clothes, until eventually I got her into her clean nappy and wrapped her in a single muslin.

When I walked into the clinic, the receptionist and I

looked at each other for a long moment, then I just said, 'Long story.' I look back now and think they probably have at least three of those a week. But that taught me the hard way to always, always, always pack extra outfits.

FIRST BABY BEAUTY TREATMENT

Top tip: don't fake tan while you're still breastfeeding. I woke up the next morning after a night feed and not only was her beautiful sleep suit covered with unnerving globs of orange-brown, but her poor face and cheeks looked like she had cartoon shaded stubble drawn on. Bottle tan is not a good look on a baby, it turns out.

FIRST HOLIDAY

After no holidays for eighteen months, we were really eager to go away during the summer of 2021 when everyone kept recommending we should travel with her while she was still a baby, and we worried lockdown restrictions could tighten again in the winter. We booked a last-minute holiday to Portugal at the start of September, and for our first holiday it took me – no joke – seven days to pack. We had to pay for extra luggage and took three enormous suitcases between the three of us. How can babies have that much stuff?

I'd dreaded the flights, but the outbound journey was a total dream. An elderly man, who'd given us a dirty look when we'd boarded the plane stopped us as he got off at the other end to say, 'Very well-behaved baby'. We found it hilarious, but she really was perfect on the way out, falling asleep drinking a bottle, sleeping most of the flight, then waking up for a cheerful and peaceful landing. It was such a great start and we were so chuffed with little Noa.

The holiday itself had its ups and downs. While it was a joy to watch Noa experience all these firsts – being on a plane, swimming in a pool, dipping her toes in the sea, feeling the sand of the beach on her fingers – Boj and I both caught norovirus and were wiped out for five days. It was a real eye-opener in how different holidays were going to be now: no longer could we lie in bed for as long as we wanted/needed, enjoying leisurely breakfasts and cocktails at sunset (when we could keep anything down). We didn't want to stay in our rooms every night, so tried to get out to a restaurant when we could, especially with my mum and dad who were there for a while, but after a few nights of Noa grabbing every piece of crockery and cutlery and throwing them to the floor, I couldn't always see the funny side. For the first time I could understand that saying about how holidays with young children aren't holidays any more, but just parenting in a different country.

The flight home couldn't have been more different from the flight out. Noa was crying, I was crying, and I'm amazed Boj didn't cry. She was crying for the first hour and forty minutes of the flight, everyone on the plane hated us, and poor Noa was in such a state that I was frantic with trying to soothe what must have been her painful ears. I'd also stupidly worn a white crepe dress on the way home, and by the time we arrived back in Britain it was covered in milk, vomit, strawberry, and vomited strawberry. It was *horrific*. When we got home I kept saying how stressful it had been. But weirdly when I look through our album from that holiday now, I want to do it all over again.

Boj has mentioned maybe going to the family version of the adult-only hotel we used to go to in Tenerife, which was just so lovely.

I said, 'But we couldn't go to the adults' bit . . . we've got Noa.'

And Boj, with infinite patience, said, 'Yes, that's why we'd be at the family bit.' I am tempted – everything feels better after a bit of sun – but I'm also well aware that holidays are more stressful when you're a parent, and I'm still reluctant to make plans since the pandemic. I might be more clued up about what to expect (and hopefully we wouldn't get norovirus again), but as she gets bigger and more mobile, that brings other complications, like ensuring stairs, pools and doors are all completely safe for toddling Noas.

We'd also like to go on holiday with Boj's mum, as we all enjoy each other's company and her dream evening (reading a book with some peace and quiet) means that Boj and I could slip out for an occasional couples' meal while Noa slept. The only trouble is that while I'd like us to spend the days round a pool in Tenerife, she'd prefer all of us to be touring the museums of Vienna and getting a bit of history and culture. I'm sure there's a happy medium somewhere – although Boj did draw the line at bringing his mother on honeymoon with us.

As Noa gets older, some travel becomes easier and some harder. At the moment, she doesn't love sitting in her car seat; the plane journey back from Portugal scarred me; and the train up to Manchester may have put me off for life. I swore I'd never be that parent giving their kid an iPad for the car, but if it keeps her happy and means we can all go to great places together, sign me up.

FIRST SWIM

We'd taken Noa into the pool in Portugal, but it was absolutely freezing so we'd abandoned that pretty sharp-ish. I found a local warm pool near us with an amazing instructor, and I thought Noa would have a meltdown getting in after her holiday experience, but she loved it. The floats, the toys, the other children and instructors – she's not about to enter the Olympics with her amazing kicking skills, but she's getting better every week and her little face when she comes up from being submerged, when her tongue darts out and keeps licking above her lip, tasting the chlorine – you can tell she loves it. It's a special time for me and her, something we do just the two of us. And, judging by how little she concentrates during lessons, I've a feeling she's going to shun lane swimming when she gets older, preferring to be one of those people who just tucks their knees up and jumps in, over and over again.

FIRST BUGGY ACCIDENT

At seven months, Noa and I had gone with the dogs for a lovely walk in our local park. We were on the path, next to a slight hill, Noa facing towards me in her buggy. I let the dogs off, and when they started running down the hill, I thought, *Let's run too*, so ran along with them, watching Noa and saying, 'Weeeeeeee!' She started cracking up, which obviously only encouraged me, and I flung myself down the hill faster and faster, all the time watching Noa's delighted face.

I'd forgotten that at the bottom of the hill was a V-shaped ditch. Instead of coming to a gentle descent or flattening out, or even taking off and landing the other side, I and the buggy went crashing full-pelt into the far side of the ditch, Noa in her buggy slid gently backwards, and I went flying above the buggy and landed the other side, hands still gripping the handlebars. Noa was hysterical with laughter at this point, which I tried to join in with, ignoring the crippling pain across my hips (which properly bruised up the next day) and the mud all over me and the buggy-hood, and was absolutely amazed, as I got up, that no one had been around to a) film it, and b) wonder why the hell I'd been taking my buggy so fast down the hill.

When I've told people that story, I am both comforted and surprised how many parents have stories like that. If you've done something similar – you're not alone.

FIRST LION KING

The Lion King is my favourite film in the whole world, so from day one of Noa's life, I have sung 'Hakuna Matata' to her, without fail, at least once a day. When she was nine months old she watched the film for the first time, and when that song came on she instantly started smiling and her face lit up. It was amazing. It's wonderful when you notice how these seeds you plant as a parent, of stuff you love, can be enjoyed by your baby too, so the whole family can share that experience together.

It was around that age too that her cuddles started to develop, when she started tucking us up together with a blanket to do nursery rhymes, or she would turn to me and be choosing to nuzzle herself into my side or under my arm, or when we'd watch something together and she'd be all excited and putting her head on my shoulder. I always love her so much, but I'd think at that moment, *I cannot wait to watch movies with you as you grow up*. It was the most amazing feeling because it was the first time she seemed to actually want to be near me, rather than just being in my arms because I picked her up.

FIRST BATHTIME MISHAP

We haven't had the best luck in the bathroom, I've got to be honest. I realised fairly early on that whenever I needed to weigh her in the early days, I needed to completely strip too – the air on their skin makes babies wee almost instantly, something I only realised after having several outfits soaked when trying to weigh Noa. The first time we put Noa in the bath, she instantly threw up milk into the water.

But it was only when she was nine months that disaster really struck in the bathroom. I mean, if there's anything that will teach a parent there is no moment too short to be distracted from a baby, it's in the bathroom, but this event meant I might never take my eyes off Noa again. I'd looked away for a moment – a *moment* – and when I looked back, still hearing her cheerful chirps and splashes, she was surrounded with these dark little marbles. *Poo*. Oh God. She was absolutely fascinated by these little nuggets that were bobbing all over the bath, turning them over in her hands.

I'd never moved so fast.

'BOOOOOOJ! WE'VE GOT POO IN THE BATH!'

I held her in my arms, dripping, but I couldn't hear Boj hurrying up the stairs. Everyone had promised us that it would happen one day, but we thought we'd escape it. Eventually, it emerged that he hadn't realised I actually wanted help – what was clear to me was, to Boj, just my usual lack of communication. Although wouldn't he even want to come and see the damage done or be weirdly fascinated at what a baby poo in the bath looks like? Maybe that's just me.

Once I'd calmed down and we'd cleaned Noa up, I asked what to do with the bath, long-term. 'I mean, I know we need to bleach it, but what if the diluted bleach stays on the bath surface and gets in Noa's eyes or mouth? We're not letting her get back in that bath. Ever. I think we need to burn it. The whole thing. It's our only option.' Boj, of course, did not allow this to happen and instead it was disinfected multiple times and left soaking in boiling water – just to make sure.

FIRST WORDS

Noa had been saying dada for *weeks* by the time she said mama at nine months old. She and I were in her nursery and my jaw just dropped, but she didn't say it again until we were driving to a Sunday lunch and she suddenly said it from her car seat. She didn't say it again for two months after that, but I knew she'd said it, and she knew it. She loved the sound of her voice from when she could first babble (I wonder where she gets that?) and watching her trying to sing along with nursery rhymes is so sweet.

When she first said mama, I thought, *If this is how I feel when she says that, what will it be like when she's actually calling me Mummy!* I don't want to wish the days away, but I know how much I'll enjoy it when she's speaking. Lots of people have warned me that you can't turn it off once they've started, even if occasionally you'd like to, but I can't wait.

FIRST CHRISTMAS

I was beyond excited about Noa's first Christmas. I loved Christmas when I was a kid, and some of my happiest memories are of waking up on Christmas morning with a present from Father Christmas at the end of our bed, and all of us going to my eldest sister Kelly's room to open them before we woke Mum and Dad. We weren't allowed into the living room until my dad had gone in and lit the fire and put the Christmas tree lights on; a CD of his favourite Christmas hits and all four of our sacks from Santa would be there, and we'd be waiting outside with the smell of the turkey Mum had cooked overnight. My dad made Santa's boot prints all over the dining room, with talcum powder for snow, and there would be bites taken out of the mince pies and carrots and most of the sherry had been drunk. It was such a special time because Mum and Dad are both only children, so every year both sets of grandparents would come to us, and we'd have a full house with all the people we loved. I couldn't wait to start building those memories with Noa.

We had some really great times in the run-up to Christmas. We went to the opening night of an Enchanted Christmas trail at a Cotswold farm, which was a night-time walk around a beautiful farm where you could feed the animals. A goat nibbled Noa's hand and she was cracking up, she loved it so much. We toasted marshmallows over a fire and stood around a huge Christmas tree, then the next morning we woke up and it was snowing. The car was about twenty metres from our lodge and even on that short journey Noa got covered with snow, and we nearly got stuck there because all these cars were trying to go up a hill on a narrow road and were just sliding straight back down. It was such a lovely Christmassy thing to do, even though Noa couldn't stand being in her car seat on the way back, and only a nursery rhyme lullaby playlist on repeat calmed her down and sent her off to sleep.

We had another nice festive experience when we took Noa to see Father Christmas for the first time at our local park in North London. The entrance of Santa's Grotto was a path with huge Christmas trees on either side, and we were greeted by two gorgeous elves on our way in, who Noa was extremely happy to see as they returned her excited waves. I was convinced she'd be scared of the big man in red, but once inside the grotto I plonked her down on a very small wooden table right in front of where Father Christmas was sitting, and she just stared at him then tried to reach for his beard. He distracted Noa by giving her a present, but she was far more interested in ringing a bell that was on the table. She wasn't fazed by him at all and even posed next to him for a few photographs (which we had framed within a matter of days). It was such a magical experience, and one I'll cherish forever.

However, Christmas Day was totally not the magical time everyone had promised – but, I suppose, in that way it went perfectly with the theme of Noa's whole 'magical first year' not being quite as advertised.

We spent 18 December with my family in a big cele-bration, all the siblings and partners and kids together. It seemed a mad gamble for my sister, who was hoping to be away on holiday for Christmas, but she said if we all kept doing lateral flow tests in the run-up, we should be OK. We were so relieved that we'd made it all the way there without any of us testing positive for COVID that we'd forgotten to worry about the threat of a stomach bug one of the kids had picked up at nursery. Despite my parents' boundaries around our norovirus in Portugal back in September (us: 'We're so unwell, can we come to your villa?', them: 'No, we don't want it here.'), neither of them thought it worth mentioning that they felt terribly sick from this bug, and that it was highly contagious. Thanks, guys! Later that day, one older guest gently vomited in the garden, apologising that they must have drunk too much (she was the most sober person there), and went home shortly after, puking her guts up.

'She's got it,' I said. 'That's the sickness bug. Who else has had it?'

Turns out my brother and his girlfriend had had it, and their daughter had been sick all week. As soon as we got home, Noa started vomiting, then got diarrhoea too; it was fully coming out both ends. Two days after that, I came home from work feeling horribly nauseous. I could only manage a few mouthfuls of soup, then I threw up all night and all the next day. Next Boj caught it, and then so did his mum, followed by his sister. Truly the magical Christmas everyone dreams of. (Of course, we also knew how lucky we were – so many other people were either completely cut off from friends and family due to positive COVID tests, or were hospitalised with far more serious problems than our stomach bug.)

It meant we couldn't spend Christmas Day with Sue as we'd planned, so we invited Boj's sister over, bought some last-minute food for a Christmas dinner, and decided we would go ahead with the plans we'd made for Christmas morning. On Christmas Eve, everyone seemed to perk up: we walked to Muswell Hill with the dogs and Noa, and did some other last-minute shopping. Noa was in a great mood. We went for mulled wine, then came home and wrapped presents next to the tree listening to Christmas songs and eating as much cheese fondue as our delicate tummies could handle. It was so relaxed and felt like Christmas was going to be great.

Then on Christmas morning, we realised just how young Noa still was when she didn't know what to do with her wrapped presents (she banged them like drums) or what to do with the strange chortling man in the big red outfit (a costumed Boj with a very handsome whitened beard). She was so shy and kept putting her head into my shoulder, but she gradually warmed to him, sitting on his knee for pictures and looking so happy.

We headed out for the Christmas Day walk on Hampstead Heath that I'd been looking forward to all year, and it rained almost non-stop, in a way that didn't feel festive in the slightest. Poor Noa started crying as we walked home, then didn't stop – she wouldn't nap, she wouldn't eat, wouldn't be comforted by our cuddles. Nothing we did could make her happy, and the only thing – the *only* thing – that would stop her crying was Mr Tumble videos. I now hate Mr Tumble. I mean, I know he's fantastic entertainment for kids, but I had dreamt so long of sharing a Christmas dinner with Noa, her enjoying her own little tiny version, and instead we all sat around the table watching Mr Tumble, on and on and on, for the rest of the day. She loves him so much and I don't blame her. He's funny, he does sign language, he's actually rather brilliant. And yet he will haunt my dreams forever. For the rest of my life, Christmas 2021 will be brought to mind every time I hear Mr Tumble, rain, or vomiting.

I'd planned such a gorgeous outfit for Noa for Christmas, and in fact she did go to my sister's wearing it for our Lawler Christmas Day on the eighteenth; it was a festive white top, red velvet bloomers, white tights and cute black slippers that looked like shoes. But the house was so hot and Noa got a juicy strawberry all down herself, so she ended up just cruising around in a babygro for most of the day.

On Christmas Day itself, she wasn't well enough to wear anything other than a soft tracksuit, and on Boxing Day at Sue's she wore a beautiful knitted red dress with a white collar and a little black bow that belonged to my niece last Christmas. The thing is . . . I hadn't exactly tried the dress on Noa beforehand. Which meant that on Boxing Day, she looked a lot like she was sporting a lovely red top over her white tights. Not that she didn't still look incredibly cute, but I did see all the Instagram shots of immaculately styled children and feel a bit guilty that I hadn't bought her first Christmas outfit myself. I styled her hair with a Christmas hairclip and resolved that next year I'd make more of an effort to have her looking fabulous on the twenty-fifth.

All three of us were so exhausted from the sickness and the lack of sleep, and then I started to go down the wormhole of comparing: looking at the Christmas pictures of everyone who'd had a baby around the same time as me, at all the happy family photos and magical moments. I had to try and make myself focus on how lucky we were, and how we'd had those nice moments before Christmas Day.

Presents-wise, I knew she wouldn't care that much, but my mum got her a little dolly that she completely loves, and we gave her a walker, on the suggestion of Siobhan, because she was standing up so much and clearly wanted a bit more stability to get around the house. It's been lovely, because that's all she did for weeks after Christmas Day, just reversing, turning around, walking up and down, and playing with the dogs as they trot beside her.

She loved the tree, too. We only managed to finish decorating it on the twenty-third, but every morning after we bought it, we'd go downstairs and turn the lights on, and Noa would wave at it, touching the branches and the baubles. I think decorating it with her next year will be really special. It can be hard as you get older and Christmases change, traditions end, but I like to think it just means you have the opportunity to start new ones. As Noa gets older, I think she'll really love hanging up stockings for Baxter and Shirley (as well as for herself), helping them open their doggy advent calendars throughout December, and sharing Christmas dinner with them. I know I can't wait.

FIRST NEW YEAR

For most of my life, New Year's Eve was *the* night of the year. When we were kids, my parents either hosted or went to house parties with their close group of friends, which meant that we'd be with the same circle of friends' kids each New Year, playing and hanging out upstairs while the parents partied below. It was so great having that as a regular thing every year, seeing each other as we grew up together and marking each midnight with the same faces. Then as I got older, it was a massive night out, with different venues and outfits and a whole gang of us planning for weeks. So that night was one of the things I worried I might miss if we had a baby.

I've got to say, it was a lot more fun than I expected, even with that one guest you always get who drinks way too much, falls into furniture, accidentally sits on one of your dogs and refuses to leave until they've found their wig from the fancy dress shop. There were only thirteen of us, but we decorated the kitchen like Studio 54 with gold streamers everywhere, and brought the decks, disco lights and lasers out, and had a great time while Noa slept through it all upstairs. My friend made us go to Costco and buy enough food for fifty, piling it into the trolley while I kept saying, 'There's only thirteen! Calm down!'

In every previous year Boj and I have been together, you'd have found us snogging each other's faces off at midnight – but this year he was poised with the confetti cannon while I DJ'd the perfect drop for the countdown at the decks. Something about that made me so sad – was it a sign of something more serious between us?

208

A few minutes later in the middle of all the chaos, we caught up and agreed that we both hoped 2021's difficulties were behind us, and we were ready for 2022 to be a huge year, with fun, marriage, fewer tears, Noa turning into a toddler, and even more adventures for our family of five. The first of January isn't always seen as that big of a milestone with a baby, but going into a whole new year with Noa for the first time felt absolutely massive all of a sudden. We'd had a tough one, and now we were looking forward with real hope.

It was such a good night, though. Boj's mum was coming over at eight the next morning, and Boj promised me we'd both get up at seven to look after Noa and clean up. Guess who actually got up, after three hours' sleep? When Sue arrived, I looked like Beetlejuice, with black rings around my eyes, trying to clean up all the confetti from the cannons we'd let off at midnight – it had got everywhere. And I mean *everywhere*. But Noa was definitely feeling better, finally over her bug, and she was great company while I cleaned up what looked like New Year's most chaotic burglary. After around four hours of cleaning, the kitchen was back to normal, and Boj stumbled downstairs for a coffee and to take care of Noa while I went back to bed for a two hour nap to feel human again. It goes to show, you can still have fun when you're a parent.

FIRST TIME AT NURSERY

I didn't feel remotely ready for Noa to start nursery in January, but I also knew that she loves other babies and would be so excited to spend time with them two days a week. She loves waving, smiling and trying to touch their faces, doing little laughs, making so much effort to engage with them and be their friend; we were at a café just before she started and she spotted twin boys around her age in highchairs at the next table, and was immediately waving at them. They were a bit fazed, but Noa then saw another baby and started waving and giggling at them instead. I knew any issue with nursery was due to my anxiety, rather than any genuine concerns about how Noa would get on; she couldn't think of anywhere better. The nursery felt perfect for her, too: we loved the staff there, the feel of the nursery, their holistic approach to how the children eat and play with different age groups, how they spend so much time outdoors no matter the weather, and get so messy every day in their exploring of the world; it's exactly the right place for Noa.

We had two induction mornings in the nursery garden, where I stayed to watch Noa settling in with the other babies and toddlers while they made chains out of sticks and Cheerios. Upon arrival the first day, Noa waved hello to everyone and the staff commented on how sociable and happy she was. She sat and watched as the other kids picked up Cheerios and hooked them on to the sticks one by one, but Noa being Noa decided to pick one up from the ground and put it in her mouth. Nobody saw but me and I remember saying quite loudly, 'Oh no, not for eating, Noa!'

Within about fifteen minutes she wanted to come back to me, and she spent the rest of the session playing with animal figurines by my side. As we were walking home, I cried at the thought of Noa spending a whole day being looked after by people I didn't know. I started to spiral, thinking, *What if that Cheerio had been a stone and she choked to death on it* – I tried my best to stop catastrophising, but my anxiety got the better of me and I arrived home feeling so confused about our decision to start her in nursery at the age of only one. Boj did his best job of reassuring me that she was being cared for by professionals, by people whose job it is to look after babies every day, and that they do a perfectly good job. I tried my hardest to stop thinking of hypothetical situations and to let the worry go.

On the second day, she really enjoyed her time in the garden and I could begin to see how happy she was and how much she'd learn and play in a way I couldn't necessarily offer her at home all the time; but I also felt that she needed just a little bit longer with us. I suppose it felt like it was her first step into the big wide world without me, and although in part that was terrifying (I had to really work to shut down the voice of anxiety in my head) and heartbreaking (how could she not mind being away from us?), it was also going to be exciting (I couldn't wait to see the friends she made) and I'm even ready to frame the first piece of 'art work' she brings home (might not frame *every* single one, though, I've gotta be honest). We pushed her start date back by six weeks and knew as soon as we did that it was the right decision for all of us. I've even given myself a mental carrot to look forward to when she has her first full day: I'll pour myself a scalding hot cup of coffee (first one in a year) and finally sort out our loft room, which over Noa's lifetime has gone from a completely bare spare bedroom into the gross Dumping Ground of Despair. That alone will make me feel about 120 per cent better.

I was doing more and more with her as she got older, but I was only one person, and I didn't know everything she needed yet. I think it's important that everyone is able to decide what works best for them, in terms of working and childcare, but I was so relieved that by the time the induction days had passed, I was totally comfortable with the idea of Noa being at nursery twice a week, and that they wouldn't mind if she ate there like she eats at home: with yoghurt going on the walls, ceiling, floor – almost anywhere except her mouth. Thanks to the staff at the nursery and my therapist Anna's advice about gradually letting myself be away from Noa in the day, she was happy, and I was happy. I already knew Noa was happy with other people as she's been cared for by her grandparents, aunts and Siobhan with no bother. Of course, I still worry – I can't imagine being away from her and not thinking about how she's doing – but she's doing so well there, digging for worms and getting paint in her hair, and it's really working for us all. Eight months ago I'd never have imagined it could have happened so smoothly.

FIRST BIRTHDAY

I know that people are free to celebrate these things however they want, but we were just so grateful to be able to mark a year of Noa's life with our families, without getting locked down with COVID, that we didn't plan anything huge. We didn't need a massive fancy event, so we just arranged a small get-together at our house with only our families and a wonderful 'Noa's Ark' cake for Noa, to mark us keeping her alive for a whole year. She'll enjoy enough children's parties (both hers and other people's) as she gets older, and at the age of one she still didn't really know what was going on, so we agreed to save a house or church hall full of kids for future birthdays. So many friends asked me what we were doing to celebrate Noa turning one and it made me realise there's an expectation to throw a big party for your child's first birthday. There were times in the month leading up to it where I began to feel guilty that we'd not organised a big event with all of our friends and their kids. It might sound bad as it's not my birthday, but it's just not what Boj or I wanted to do. Then I reminded myself that Noa probably won't hold it against us, given that she probably won't remember what happened on 11 February 2022 when she's older. When she was eight months, it seemed like the longest year of my life, but at her birthday celebrations it felt like the whole year had swept by in a flash. For her birthday present, we took her to Whipsnade Zoo, since she's obsessed with animals. I, of course, worried that a rhinoceros would somehow get out of the enclosure and eat her, but we managed to avoid that and she was amazed that all these things she'd only ever seen on TV were now sniffing and hooting and pacing only metres away from her. I'm so glad we went.

When I look back on her first year, so much has changed, but also so much is exactly the same. I was putting healing gel on my section scar, and suddenly remembered showing it to the health visitor just after Noa's birth – now I look at it and can't imagine how they got my gorgeous growing girl out of such a tiny incision! And at a year, I could no longer stand and rock Noa to sleep if she woke up in the middle of the night crying, but had to sit in the rocking chair with her leaning on me; I remember just how tiny she felt on my chest when she was lifted out of me in theatre.

I don't want to look too far into the future and dream about Noa as a grown-up, but the fact is that I'm so excited about every step she'll take: walking, running, climbing, talking to us, new friends, new skills, new tastes. And speaking of new tastes, it's not just Noa's that have changed over the last year: just before her birthday the three of us were watching Mr Tumble videos, Boj and I rolling our eyes at each other as Mr Tumble tried to make a den with two chairs and a coat. It was time for Noa's bath, but neither of us went to turn the TV off.

Boj turned to me. 'How would you feel if I said I wanted to see how the den is going to turn out?'

And I said, 'Mate, same.'

Mr Tumble! How did that happen? As I may have mentioned, I hated Mr Tumble. But I suppose times change . . .

I remember how difficult the first soft play session was that I ever took Noa to. I'd arrived late, she couldn't crawl like many of the other babies, she was crying, I was stressed thinking everyone was judging me, I left too late so Noa got hungry in the car and cried again, then had a meltdown when we got home. But six months on, when we went again, it was great! She was enjoying herself so much, laughing with the other babies, I was so much more confident about my abilities as a mum, that I could care for Noa and give her what she needed, and we both had a great time. I wasn't bothered that other children were walking – Noa could wave, and clap, and smile widely when she recognised songs that were being sung, and I could see that every child learns at a different pace. But all that took time, for both me and Noa, and for me to see that she is her own person, and Boj and I are just there to love and support her, however she needs, without putting massive pressure on ourselves. It amazes me how much I'm enjoying being a mum these days; for so long, I was convinced I would feel depressed and regretful and a failure and incompetent forever, yet at the end of the first year I feel blissful just caring for and loving Noa – tired, but happy just being her mum.

In the last few weeks before she turned one, I found myself constantly watching her – when she was asleep, or absorbed in touching everything she could in our kitchen while whizzing around in her little walker, or giggling with the dogs – and watching videos of her as a newborn. How was she that small? How is she just about walking, chattering to us, bringing us things, making us laugh? I'm still not remotely broody for another one (I told Boj the other day that I was thinking of getting my tubes tied, but he just rolled his eyes at me), but every single day it's clear that she's becoming a proper person, not just a gorgeous baby. She's got jokes with us now – that if we say a particular word, she'll start fake coughing, then fake sneezing, then doing a fake laugh that means we all end up cracking up. She's just amazing, and continues to become more amazing every day.

FIRST WEDDING

It's been a real rollercoaster organising this wedding, I have to say. Even without wanting it to be a huge fancy thing, events of the last two years have made it trickier; we still haven't seen the venue, because the hotel closed down during the height of the pandemic, was taken over and then refurbished. I tried on fifty dresses and finally found one I liked, so when I put it on recently and felt a bit over it, there was no way I was going to start dress hunting again. Noa and my niece will now be the flower girls on the day, which my mum got really emotional about. My friend who is ordained will be marrying us in a star-spangled banner catsuit, then we'll have a party for everyone and finally be married. We've still got a few things to do, like rings and bridesmaid dresses, booking a honeymoon and buying Baxter a tuxedo, but my main concerns are that my dad is well enough to walk me down the aisle, and that Noa has a happy day in whatever cute dress she's wearing. I still can't believe she'll be walking down the aisle too – that she'll be with us for this amazing day. She probably won't remember anything about it when she's older, but there will be enough photos for her to see how important she was to it all. I know that her smile, and maybe her little fake coughs and sneezes, are going to light up the whole day.

I mean it, I *don't* want to wish any time away, ever, and I'm beginning to understand how quickly it can go and how precious it is, but I also have this sense that the wedding has been put on hold for so long that I just want us to be married. Once we're married, we can finally get on with our lives, the five of us, and enjoy Noa growing up. First the wedding was postponed, then I was pregnant, then we were caring for Noa – and now that she's reached her first birthday, we're past that point that always seemed like it would be the trickiest. So now Noa is one, and the pandemic is passing, and once we're married, things will go back to like feeling like they're normal again. Right?

Right?

FIRST . . . SIBLING?

Sometimes I'm asked by – clearly very, very brave – people, if I'd ever have another baby. There's a simple answer to that:

Abso-fucking-lutely not.

I'm forty-two soon, which isn't exactly the easiest age to get pregnant, and my eggs aren't getting any fresher. I'll be fifty when Noa's ten, I still can't imagine going to pick her up from school and looking around at all the other mums in the playground as I know I'll be thinking, *Am I the oldest one here?* Not that it matters, but I'm constantly reminded that I left it late to have baby number one, let alone a second. The fertility clinic also already told us my eggs were nearly done a couple of years ago. Although when perimenopause hits, I know that can cause a real spike in broodiness and fertility – the eggs are like, 'Last gasp. Go, go, go. Last gasp. Everyone out!'

I also know that I *never* wanted a baby, and I *never* thought things with Noa would get better. Too many mums have said to me, 'I only ever wanted one, until that one got to twelve months,' for me to think I'm above ever wanting another, but right now it's a hard 'No thank you, I love Noa and one is definitely enough.' Boj and I are more experienced now, we're more confident about our own abilities as parents. I've gone from someone who never even wanted to hold a baby, to someone whose highlight of their day is Noa simultaneously burping and trumping in front of me. And when she started smiling at me . . . it was the most magical feeling; my heart could have burst. When your baby gets to the age where you can make them laugh, and even better, they can make *you* laugh – there honestly isn't anything better in the whole world.

But right now, it already feels like we have three human children, and the house is always a mess, and I'm still constantly tired, and I don't feel like I ever have time to do even a fraction of the stuff that's on my To Do list. I'd like to continue renovating our home, which we put on hold once Noa arrived; we need to do the bathroom, the downstairs toilet, and the kitchen, and we need a new sofa, decent blinds, and the more babies there are, the longer we have to put that off. I miss Noa so much when I'm not with her, but that's also a reason to stick with just her: do I want to be in an even more chaotic home, and missing two babies when I'm away from them, instead of one? And do I feel a little bit sad that she won't have Christmases and holidays like I did, with loads of siblings? Maybe, but all year round Noa has Baxter and Shirley, she has her cousins, she has all our friends' babies to see on playdates, so it's not like she's living on an island with only me and Boj for company. And for every only child who wishes their parents had had more children, there are children who wish desperately that they hadn't had siblings, that the siblings disrupted their childhood and they aren't close as adults, and having a brother or sister added nothing to their lives. (I only discovered recently that Boj and his sister always got presents on the other one's birthday, just so they didn't get upset about being 'left out'. I now like to wind Boj up and say that he was a little diva child.) Shirley and Baxter may have ignored her the very first time they met her, but they now have the most incredible bond with Noa – Baxter understood how special she was from the very beginning, and would often just be sitting watching her in her crib – and she finds them so funny, Baxter rolling over to have his tummy tickled and Shirley licking Noa's ears. Plus, Noa has realised that, at mealtimes, if she holds her hands down the dogs will lick them clean, or she can pass them anything she doesn't want. They are her brother and sister, they just have more legs and a bit more hair.

Every day that Noa gets older, it's nice to think about the things we can do together in the future, things that we couldn't do or might have to wait much longer for if she had a sibling. Before any babies were in the picture, we had visions of a romantic getaway to the Seychelles for our honeymoon, but now our plans look slightly different. We'll chill at home for a few days after the wedding, the five of us, then just me and Boj will go away for five nights to Lake Como to relax, then fly home, collect Noa, Baxter and Shirley and head off for a two-week road trip around France. Before Noa starts school it's the perfect chance, when she'll be excited about seeing and doing new things (and watching Mr Tumble on an iPad in the car), and this will be the best opportunity for me and Boj, even though everyone thinks we're bananas for doing it. I mean, when has anyone's advice ever stopped us before?

Boj has always wanted more than one, and I never wanted any, so is one the compromise? A really upsetting message I once had online was from someone who said, 'Please have another baby, because an only child is a lonely child!' I wrote back, saying, 'I'm sure you didn't mean to offend me, but it's really not cool to say that to a parent,' and we ended up having a good conversation about it.

Boj and I still talk about it too, and he asked me recently if I ever feel sad that Noa is such a sociable baby and won't have any siblings. I had to admit that for the first time, I did actually feel a bit sad about it, but I also know that there are no guarantees that she'd definitely get on with any siblings, that they wouldn't be fighting all day every day and total opposites in every way possible. So, we can't have another baby just to keep Noa occupied, and besides, she'll have more playdates and friends over than anyone, I reckon, as well as having her amazing bond with Baxter and Shirley.

In fact, Boj, who wanted multiple children, now says he can't ever watch me go through all that again and go back to that dark place. I was sorting out all Noa's clothes to pass on the other day, and I asked Boj what he'd say if I suddenly suggested having another. He just said, 'Nope.' Mums might forget how bad things were, but I don't think their partners ever do. But what suits one family might not suit another, and the idea that I'm letting Noa down because I don't want to risk feeling like that again, suicidal and broken, is *so* wrong. Women get pressure from all directions about having babies or not having babies, the right time and the wrong time, when really the only right choice is the one you make.

A word with . . . Boj (The Handsome)

I pretty much knew that Kate was the woman I wanted to spend the rest of my life with from the day I met her. And I knew that if she truly decided that she didn't want to have kids, then I'd rather live the rest of my life with her than meet someone else and have children with them. It was always Kate first.

When she said we should try for children, I didn't really believe it, if I'm totally honest. Over the years, I'd always said we should think about it, not least because I always knew what a fantastic mum she was to the dogs and how she has this natural warmth, and I had this feeling that she'd make an amazing mum. But I couldn't make her, she had to want to. Sometimes I felt like she really entrenched her position of *I don't want kids* because it was something she'd said early on, and it was hard for her to flip back on that because it was such a big part of her personality. We'd have these discussions and she'd say, 'OK, in January, why don't we start trying?' And then January comes, and she'd not be ready yet, but I was always patient. The podcast episode when we went to the fertility clinic brought it home to her, and something changed, so when she said we should try, I thought we should just take advantage of the moment in case she changed her mind the next morning, because she'd done that before. I'd learned not to get too excited when she said yes and not to get too depressed when she said no.

I think part of the problem was Kate's fear of commitment, and also her conviction that I'd leave her, even though we've been together so long, and it isn't something I can really do anything about. And trying for a baby is a battlefield of its own – we were so lucky not to have to go through what some couples go through on those journeys, with miscarriages and IVF, and all the grief that can come with that basic human instinct to have a child. If we'd struggled to conceive, then maybe she would have changed her mind. In fact, it was lucky it worked first time because she would in all likelihood have changed her mind again the next day.

When Kate told me it was a girl, with her Cornettos, honestly, I was so happy. I just wanted our baby to be healthy and to come out, and that was it. I didn't care, boy or girl – whatever we had, that baby would watch football with me.

Apparently this is really common, but the first person I told about the baby was a mate who I'm not even that close to. I think I just wanted to tell someone, but someone who wasn't right in the middle of our lives, and telling him made it feel that bit more real. Telling our parents, though – they were all so shocked, but eventually they descended on us, my mum hugging Katie, it was so special.

For the birth, I was lucky that we were a bit later in the pandemic, because any earlier and I wouldn't have been allowed in at all. It was slightly stressful for a while, when they were pushing Kate to have a vaginal birth, and I was all ready to bang on the doors and make a scene, but thankfully they probably ignored me and took us up soon afterwards to get ready for Kate's surgery. The birth was amazing, and the team really had all their shit together (which you'd hope, obviously), and it was so reassuring. I spent the whole time chatting to Kate, until it was time for Noa to come out and I could see they were really *yanking*, and I was thinking, *Is this normal? Should I say something?* but then they brought Noa out and held her up.

My god, she was so swollen and squished up. I don't know what I was expecting, but I wasn't expecting that! She was clearly so unhappy at being removed like that, which you can understand – you're not going to look your best at that moment. But she was also totally gorgeous. They put her on Kate, and we had this moment, the three of us, and I was crying, and I'll always remember that, our little swollen, alien baby. We took a photo in the recovery room, when we were so happy, and we all look absolutely knackered.

And then Noa was in and out of hospital, and it was quite a tough first twelve weeks, emotionally. But you also adapt quite quickly, because this is your first experience of a baby it becomes normal.

When I saw the impact of it on Kate it was really hard because I didn't know what to do. She always internalises her problems and won't say anything until the very last minute, and she was basically having a breakdown. I was trying to do as much as I could, but Kate felt that she had to do everything herself, to be a perfect mum, and she didn't want to relinquish any control and be seen as a failure.

The breastfeeding wasn't going well, and Noa was struggling to latch, and one night I was asleep and Kate came in, both her and Noa really crying, and I suddenly realised that I needed to intervene, I had to stop trying to avoid telling Kate what to do. I told her we needed help, and that she needed to sleep. Neither of us knew what we were doing, so to have someone come in and say, 'You're not doing a bad job, let's do these things to help', was an absolute lifeline. Kate was trying so hard to stay independent, and I felt an immense amount of guilt that I was watching her struggle, and still feel guilt that I leave the house to go to work, that I leave everything on her.

It's amazing watching Noa grow – we quickly forget the different stages she's been through, how she's gone from being this tiny thing with so little awareness, to sitting up, standing up, so sharp and full of different emotions. I just love it, seeing her grow and develop in these leaps.

Fatherhood has its challenges, but I wouldn't change it at all. I don't think I was particularly selfish before, but parenthood means that you are on the clock, permanently, with no breaks, really, and no free time, and it's all-encompassing. The flip side is that you have this new person and you'll do absolutely anything to make them laugh, and I find myself sitting with her just wanting to cry at how much I love her. But I also still think, *Who are you? Where did you come from?* She's this whole other person! It's very strange, but it's wonderful.

My advice for any partners is to accept that the first six months will be hard, and to be there for the baby and mum as much as you can. A mum might be so stressed and sleep-deprived that she doesn't always know what they need, so you have to be that extra pair of eyes to spot things she can't at that time. It's also good to be the filter between what family might be trying to advise, and what your partner needs – family support is so important, but their opinions might not always align with what your new family wants to do. As a new parent you need patience, support, and above all, a sense of humour. There's no point in trying to fight against the things that are happening to you. You may as well try to embrace it and, as far as you can, enjoy it.

I love how Boj still believes I spent years claiming I didn't want kids because I'm too stubborn to go back on my word. Think we'll have to just agree to disagree on that one. When I think back to the first nine months (the first six especially) of us being parents, I realise how much of a rock he was and how lucky I am that one of us knows the importance of conversation. The pep talks he gave me when he could sense that I was feeling lost or stressed, they gave me the strength to get through each day. I'll never forget how he helped me through the hardest period of my life. I don't think I'd have got through those days without him.

But the stress of Christmas, of illness, our own and Noa's, meant that Boj and I started arguing. He felt like we weren't in a good place, but it meant we had another heart-to-heart and started sessions with our couples' therapist again, and I booked back in with Anna. I even switched from the CBD oils to taking the medication I'd been given a month before, although I should have learned my lesson from 2018. Back then I'd moved from a job I didn't love, which was away from all my friends and family, to my dream job in London near to everyone I loved. It triggered a depressive episode that only lifted a year later when I finally took the citalopram prescribed by my doctor. I was on it for six months, after which I slowly weaned myself off it, once I was stable and managing again; I've discussed with my therapist why it's only when my life is going well that I seem to have these depressions, and her theory is that I get crushed by the fear of losing all the good things I have at that time.

So when this happened again – back at work doing a job I loved, Noa sleeping and growing well, a home I loved with a man I loved – I finally realised I needed to take the citalopram again, and at least this time I didn't wait a full year to do it. I had to give up the CBD oil as you can't take the two together, but the oil is something I think I'll go back to in the future when I'm generally in a better place, as it did help with sleep and heart palpitations.

It also showed me that I *still* have the attitude of 'I can do this alone, I don't need help, I don't need medication, I'm "strong enough" to fix this all on my own,' which, I've learned from the last year, is total rubbish: no one can do that on their own. Taking the citalopram didn't mean I wasn't a good enough person, or partner, or mum – it didn't *mean* anything. It was just medication, and it's there for a reason, and if you need it, and can find the right one for you, it can be a lifesaver. Taking medication that a doctor has prescribed you should never make you feel like a 'failure'. I need to keep being aware that life will throw me difficult times, and that, in those times, I have to be able to recognise that I'm struggling and remember what helps me get through. And I'm a massive backer of therapy for everyone; if you can access it in any way, online or in person, by phone or chat, please do it. You might feel uncomfortable or embarrassed in that first session, but you'll also realise that a weight is gradually being lifted off your shoulders when you find the right therapist.

Boj and I, like most couples, need the tools and support to get through stressful stages, but it was only when our therapist asked us to describe our lives over the last few years that we saw how much we'd been through: it's likely that Noa's start in life has meant that any illness makes us react much more strongly and more stressfully than we need to; then 2021 saw Boj being made redundant and starting his own business; I headed back to work, trying to be a mother, a radio presenter, and also taking on a lot more work on social media; we had our wedding cancelled; plus family illnesses; and a global pandemic (in case you hadn't noticed that one). It has been a stressful time, and both of us feel like we want to find our way again, ready for our wedding and starting our marriage on the right foot.

At the moment, Boj is great at communicating while I still struggle, but in our therapy sessions I can say what I'm feeling. In that environment I don't worry that it

will cause an argument. Our therapist makes us describe any disagreement from the other person's point of
view, which allows us to see how we can actually solve
any problem we have, that any argument we think we're
having is very rarely what's actually going on. We're
still learning how to be parents together, and how to
make each other happy as a couple, but I'm so glad Boj
is willing to work on it too, because these are the most
important things: making our family happy together
and being able to talk about whatever needs sharing.

That said, there are still bad days, like in January 2022
when Boj and I had quite a bad argument which ended
with me breaking down in tears explaining how tired
and sad I'd been feeling. I'd taken on far too much work
(including writing this book) and I honestly felt like I
was at breaking point. I was also acutely aware that it
had been a while since Boj and I had had any time to
ourselves, so the plan had been to have an early night
(if you know what I mean). We'd watched an episode
of our favourite show and I thought we'd then head
upstairs for some fun, so when he suggested watching
Curb Your Enthusiasm, I lost it, feeling rejected, like
he'd rather have Larry David over me. Combined with
the fact that I'd been focusing on everything else in my
life except Boj, it felt like our relationship was being
neglected. Thankfully, we had an honest and lengthy

conversation and made up, and the following evening enjoyed a lovely long hot bath with candles, some of our favourite songs and a really nice time in bed . . . with no Larry David.

The people in this book really did save me. They were honest and caring, supportive and listening, and didn't let anything get in the way of me as a new mum having what was needed to care for our baby.

I wish more people could have warned me how terrible it could be at the beginning, but for every parent who struggled like me there'll be one where it was a dream, and the easiest stage of parenting, and they have no idea what I'm talking about. But I remember my friend Kate being on speaker phone shortly before I gave birth, saying, 'Listen: the first twelve weeks are mental, do what you can to survive,' and we thought at the time that her over-dramatic words were hilarious. Ellie Taylor had also been really honest about how hard she found the first year, but I had no idea how bad I'd feel until it happened to me. It's such a personal experience; you always think your own go will be totally different to everyone else's, but there's always going to be some overlap. And maybe other parents just didn't want to scare me.

We need honest conversations about how hard that first year can be for mums and dads, not that it will be, but that it could be – and around the things that can help: social and professional support, a bit of time and space for a mum to take care of herself or have a rest, better knowledge of a baby's feeding and sleeping needs, and much more expert breastfeeding support for every single woman. I wish I'd had the courage to ask for help sooner, for my sake and for Noa's. I wish that I'd cut myself a bit more slack, and understood that we don't have to be alone. And I wish that someone had told me earlier that the frills of a nappy have to face outwards. It would have saved a lot of nappies and a *lot* of stained vests and babygros. HOW could I have known that?

I hope this is one honest conversation that might help people, whether it's looking forward at possible futures, or back at past situations we've stumbled through. It's not the *only* conversation, it's not necessarily the conversation that will fit you and your choices best, but this book is an honest look at the ways we all struggle, learn, and love, far beyond what we ever thought possible. Good luck, with whatever you choose.

Letter to Noa
(on her first birthday)

To my darling Noa,

From today, your age will no longer be measured in days, weeks or months but in years that I know will go as quickly as the last. I want to say first and foremost how much I love you and can't ever imagine living without you. You light up my life in more ways than I could ever have hoped for, my precious and perfect little potato. When you were lifted from my tummy that afternoon of 11 February 2021 and into my arms, you filled my head with emotions I'd never felt before and my heart with a love that grows stronger every day.

When you're old enough to read this book, I hope you understand the importance of Mummy telling her story and that by sharing the details of my first year as your mum, my aim was to try and help other new or expectant parents. Despite my struggles, it was never you who made me sad, I was just frustrated with myself for finding the first eight months so difficult.

You have no idea how much you've amazed me already. You're smart, kind, funny, loving and beautiful. Your smile lights up a room and you have the most beautiful blue eyes I've ever seen. You're already the best little sister to Baxter and Shirley, who love you so, *so* much. I can't wait to take you on adventures with them and to watch you become the trio of best friends I know you're destined to be.

This year, 2022, is such a big year for you, Tayto. You've had your first birthday, and started your steps to nursery too. I am so excited for you to make your very first friendships and become independent as you learn.

The thought of you watching Mummy and Daddy get married later this year gives me butterflies, Noa. You are going to look like a little angel, walking down the aisle as my flower girl. Our wedding was cancelled and delayed by two years due to the pandemic, but every cloud has a silver lining: now we get to have you there with us.

Although it's only been a year, it's been the most incredible journey watching you grow and change, and I already know you'll grow up to be the most beautiful, charismatic and wonderful person. There are so many things I can't wait for, like your first day at school, finding out what subjects you enjoy and watching you on Sports Day. Will you be academic like your dad, or creative and sporty like your mum? I already know I'm going to be a bit sad when you move out, or head off to university – to even try and imagine what you'll look like and who you'll be dating or what you'll be into is impossible! All I hope is that you have at least one loving and loyal friend, and you don't get into too much trouble.

I wonder what your first job will be, where your career will take you, if you'll follow in your mummy's footsteps and work in radio? Wouldn't it be marvellous if you weren't terrified of flying like I am and you become a pilot?! (Please don't become a pilot, I will never sleep again.) I predict you will have at least one dog as you're already so confident and loving around Baxter, Shirley and every dog you meet. I promise to dog-sit whenever you need me.

I hope the world is a much safer and kinder place when you're a grown woman and you feel safe wherever you go, that you'll visit all the countries your mum and dad didn't get to and explore everywhere we did as well. I want you to experience different cultures and land-scapes, discovering as much of the planet as you possibly can. What if you travel somewhere and you want to stay? (Why am I putting this idea into your head?) I hope wherever you end up living in the world, no matter how long you're there, you'll always remember your mum and dad and you'll want to stay in touch with us. I cannot imagine not speaking to you for more than a day – I mean, look at me now, you're a one-year-old and I still can't bring myself to leave you overnight! I wonder how we'll keep in touch? Will FaceTime still be a thing? Will you have a microchip in your eye that connects to mine the moment you say, 'Call Mum'?

Whatever person you grow up to be, whichever career path you decide on, whoever you choose to date, I will support you. I remember introducing my first boyfriend to your grandad, who shook the guy's hand so hard he nearly broke his fingers. Naughty Grandad. I promise not to be as intimidating as Grandad Des to anyone you date or bring home, Tayto.

Only do what makes you happy, be brave, be kind and always remember there is no problem too big that you can't ask me for help. I can't promise to know all the answers but I'm always here as a shoulder to cry on, and I'll make you cheese on toast when you have a bad day.

I hope you have a lifetime of happiness, and I promise you now and always that there will never be a shortage of love around you. Thank you for teaching me to be more patient, that our mental health is as important as our physical health and that it's OK to ask for help. I've always believed the meaning of life is to be happy, so as Henry David Thoreau once said: Go confidently in the direction of your dreams! Live the life you've imagined.

Happy first birthday, Noa. I'm so lucky I get to be your mum. x

Kate's Top Tips

TEN THINGS I NOW REALISE EVERY PARENT SHOULD KNOW.

Hindsight is such a wonderful thing, isn't it? But if I can't learn all this for my first baby, hopefully these tips might help someone else:

1. Newborns make so much noise in their sleep. My goodness, the first night Noa slept in her nursery instead of the crib next to my bed was the best night's sleep I'd had since she was born.
2. It can take ages to wind a newborn baby. I spent *hours* walking around the house trying to get a burp out of Noa after feeds.

3. Get a baby bouncer sooner rather than later. Noa still loved being in hers at eleven months – the shape and the gentle rocking sensation are really soothing for your baby, perfect to pop them in while you shower or do some housework. I didn't buy one for some time.

4. Learn to use a sling before the baby arrives. This means you can have your little one comfortably snuggled against you instead of carrying them and trying to do housework with one hand.

5. Ask for help or hire a doula sooner, instead of waiting until you hit rock bottom.

6. Dummies are OK! I don't know why I resisted. It soothes and it's totally safe for newborns to have one (and if they don't want it, don't keep trying to force it on them!).

7. Make parenting your only job in those first six months if you can – I was doing brand work on Instagram because I didn't get any paid maternity leave from my radio job, and I always worry about money so felt I had no choice.

8. Research how to keep milk supply up if you want to breastfeed. I focused on positioning and latching techniques but if I'd read more about what affects milk supply, the best times to express and what can help our bodies with supply, then perhaps I'd have

kept my milk supply high instead of it dwindling because of what I was and wasn't doing.

9. Accept that a fed baby is a happy baby. You can bond with your baby in so many ways, not just from breastfeeding. Formula or boob fed, they all end up eating McDonalds French fries off the floor by the time they're four.

10. You can never take too many photos. I don't have many photos of me and Noa together during the first year. I have tons of her, and of Boj and her, but not so many of her and me. I'll treasure the few we have!

TEN ITEMS I'D RECOMMEND FOR FIRST-TIME PARENTS

You'll be given a thousand soft toys and thirty copies of *The Very Hungry Caterpillar*, but these are the things that genuinely make useful gifts for parents making their way through that first year:

1. A comfortable feeding chair. We ordered ours *way* too late and for the first five weeks I could never get comfortable feeding Noa in our bed; I used to go into the nursery for night feeds and sit on the floor with my back against a giant unicorn teddy! Not fun.

Once the rocking chair arrived and I was able to feed in comfort, it was a game changer.

2. The Tommy Tippee Perfect Prep machine (for formula-fed babies). We spent ages when we began using formula popping the bottle in a jug of boiling water and waiting for everything to heat up and cool down.

3. The Love To Dream Newborn Swaddle Up. Way easier to use than traditional swaddles because they have a zip, and from the moment we put Noa in one, she slept better.

4. A SnoozeShade for the pram. Breathable and safe to use in the summer so they can sleep and be protected from the sunshine and insects while out on walks during the day.

5. The White Noise Deep Sleep app, which is free to download. A plethora of soothing sounds to calm your baby to sleep.

6. Rockit Baby Rocker. We used to place ours underneath her mattress in the Moses basket to help get her to sleep.

7. A soft chunky knit comforter. Noa loved having something to nuzzle into and we used a muslin until I saw @thelittlebabyhut and her gorgeous comforters on Instagram. Tip: always buy a couple in case you lose one.

8. Vanish powder stain remover. I wish I'd discovered it before Noa was ten months old, I'd probably have ended up with far fewer permanently stained clothes.
9. *Hey Bear Sensory* on YouTube, and the *Black on White* book by Tana Hoban. When Noa was really young she was mesmerised watching this and looking at the book, which I'd lay beside her changing mat.
10. My Pura newborn nappies that come with a yellow line which turned blue when the nappy was wet. Some newborn nappies don't have this line, and it's very handy.

TEN TIPS FOR HOLIDAYING ABROAD WITH A BABY

I can't tell you how much extra junk we packed on that first holiday; we could have started a baby shop out there. Here are the ten things that really do make a difference on a trip far from home:

1. A fan you can attach to the pram – an essential one for sun holidays. Noa would have melted without this, and they're easily adaptable to most prams.
2. Wipe-down silicone bibs (instead of cloth ones) – wherever you are, you can wipe it down or rinse it

off and pop it straight back in your bag, ready for the next meal.

3. A SnoozeShade for the travel cot – helps keep your baby cool and shaded for napping, whatever the time of day.

4. A SnoozeShade for your pram – keeps the strong sun off your baby's delicate skin, and means they can nap as you walk about through the day.

5. A NUK baby-food masher and bowl – easy to clean and suitable for any baby food, easy to pop in your bag for any café stop-offs with your little one.

6. Extra bottles of formula for take-off and landing – the sucking sensation helps with potentially sore popping ears, and the milk comforts them and hopefully puts them to sleep.

7. Ask the hotel if they provide sterilisers before packing one – many hotels offer this service and it'll save you so much luggage room.

8. Download nursery rhymes or baby sensory playlists on your phone – wherever you are, you'll have a comforting sound for your baby to be soothed by.

9. Take familiar books/toys with you – even if your baby is experiencing fantastic new things in wild new places, the comfort of reliable books and toys (just a few) is worth the extra space.

10. Don't pack loads of baby clothes – it's tempting to

load up with delicious new holiday outfits, but if you're going somewhere warm they might actually need fewer than normal. Noa spent most of her time in a nappy during the day in Portugal.

TEN TIPS FOR COUPLES WHO ARE FIRST-TIME PARENTS

It's never going to be a walk in the park, but it doesn't have to be terrible. It can even be fun! (Sometimes.) Here's how to keep the love going:

1. Communicate with one another. As someone who still struggles to articulate how I'm feeling, I remember all too well how we'd fall out a lot during the newborn days because I'd bottle everything up, which would end up causing an argument. Going to sleep after a row was always painful, but since learning to be more open and talk about things, we argue less and always make up before going to sleep. There really is nothing like a sorry, a kiss and a cuddle, and then sleeping in the same bed.
2. Try and have a sense of humour. The first month will be terribly difficult, you're both going to be more tired than you've ever been before and although it

might not feel like there is a lot to laugh about, if you can see the funny side of little disasters, it really helps.

3. What happens today probably won't happen tomorrow, almost definitely won't happen in a month, and you'll have forgotten about it happening in a year. Try not to get too ground down about the situation now, as everything is a phase.

4. Find some time just for the two of you. Everyone's priorities change when a baby comes along, but it doesn't change the fact that you chose to have one together, so make sure you try and keep that bond as strong as possible.

5. Find things to do together that have nothing to do with the baby. As simple as starting a new series on TV that you can enjoy and discuss to take your mind off being new parents, for even just an hour.

6. Split tasks. Doing everything together may seem like a good idea (and is for many things) but eventually you'll realise that by splitting the tasks, you'll be able to give the other person a rest.

7. Accept that you're both going to make mistakes. Don't get bogged down in who did what wrong, you're both going to be tired and frazzled and as a new parent you are constantly learning, so it's inevitable, just accept and it and move on.

8. Talk to other parents about how they got through the first year. When the other person is driving you mad, it will help to know that it's completely normal for relationships to suffer after having a baby and you can get through it. Ask other mums or dads what they did to keep their relationship on track.

9. Don't feel guilty about having less sex during the first year. I've run three marathons and after each one I was *exhausted*. If Boj had tried it on after them I'd have told him to get lost. My point here is that one day of parenting a newborn is more tiring than running a marathon so you might want to sleep instead of having sex. It doesn't mean you're not attracted to one another or that the relationship is breaking down. Just give yourself some time.

10. From Boj: as a dad, no matter what you were doing before the baby came along, if you're ever in doubt about what you need to do, get up and do *something* to help around the house. Wash up, tidy up, put the bins out, hang the washing, put another load of laundry on, make some food; it's going to be full-on, but it gets easier.

Acknowledgements

Thanks to Orion Books and to the lovely Sam Binnie for help polishing my story. Thanks to Becca, Jack and everyone at Becca Barr Management for your love and support. Thanks to Mike Cass and Virgin Radio for giving me the opportunity to get better and spend more time with my daughter before returning to work. Thanks to Siobhan and Emiliana, for all of your words of wisdom and support during pregnancy, birth and beyond. Thanks to each and every one of the NHS staff at the Whittington hospital for taking such good care of us all, and especially Noa. We are so lucky and grateful for the compassionate and hardworking individuals in the NICU and during our A&E visits.

Kate Sinnott, thank you for keeping your phone on loud so I could call or text in the middle of the night when I went into labour and during the first few months when I was worried or had a question. Thanks to every single one of my friends, and there are too many of you to name individually, but you've all helped me navigate the toughest year of my life so far. The calls, texts, door-step visits and socially distanced walks: I am so lucky to be surrounded by such a kind and caring bunch of humans. To every person who makes up the greatest online friendship group I could wish for on Instagram, your messages, love and support normalised how I was feeling and gave me the strength to keep going.

To Sue, for all of your help, I don't know what we'd do without you. To my twin sister, Karen, for making such an effort to help us every single week for a whole year; I know how long the commute is but Noa absolutely loves you and I know the journeys are worth it. Thanks to my little brother, Rob, and Tanya for all of your advice and for lending us so much baby paraphernalia. To big sister Kelly and sister-in-law Eva for being amazing aunties.

To my mum and dad, who for so long believed I'd never have children, I am so glad I gave you another granddaughter. You have both welcomed her into your lives with such warmth and love and she's so lucky to have you as grandparents. Thank you for giving me the best childhood memories and showering us with love and affection. It's all I ever needed and I love you both for keeping our family together always.

Lastly, thank you to Boj. Your kindness, patience and resilience, especially over the past year, continues to amaze me. I always knew you'd be a wonderful father and I can't wait for all the adventures to come with Noa, Baxter and Shirley. You're like a life-coach, personal chef and fiancé in one, how lucky am I to have found you? You really do have no idea how much I appreciate all the sacrifices you've made for us.

About the Author

Presenter, podcaster and mother Kate Lawler shot to fame after winning the third series of *Big Brother UK* in 2002, making her the first ever female winner of the reality TV hit.

Since then, Kate has carved out a successful media career, as both a presenter and guest across a range of popular TV and radio shows. In 2016 she moved to Virgin Radio, where she has been hosting the drive-time show since 2019.

In 2019, Kate and her partner Boj launched their award-winning and chart-topping podcast, *Maybe Baby*, to open up discussions around the decision to have children. With rave reviews and over 1 million listens to date, *Maybe Baby* has been praised for tackling a taboo subject in a relatable and entertaining way.

A year later, Kate and Boj decided to try for a baby and, in February 2021, Kate gave birth to her first child, a daughter whose name is Noa. This is Kate's first book.

Help us make the next generation of readers

We – both author and publisher – hope you enjoyed this book. We believe that you can become a reader at any time in your life, but we'd love your help to give the next generation a head start.

Did you know that 9 per cent of children don't have a book of their own in their home, rising to 13 per cent in disadvantaged families*? We'd like to try to change that by asking you to consider the role you could play in helping to build readers of the future.

We'd love you to think of sharing, borrowing, reading, buying or talking about a book with a child in your life and spreading the love of reading. We want to make sure the next generation continue to have access to books, wherever they come from.

And if you would like to consider donating to charities that help fund literacy projects, find out more at **www.literacytrust.org.uk** and **www.booktrust.org.uk**.

THANK YOU

*As reported by the National Literacy Trust